Y0-AFJ-475

Palgrave Studies in Religion, Politics, and Policy

Series Editors: Ted G. Jelen and Mark J. Rozell

A generation ago, many social scientists regarded religion as an anachronism, whose social, economic, and political importance would inevitably wane and disappear in the face of the inexorable forces of modernity. Of course, nothing of the sort has occurred; indeed, the public role of religion is resurgent in US domestic politics, in other nations, and in the international arena. Today, religion is widely acknowledged to be a key variable in candidate nominations, platforms, and elections; it is recognized as a major influence on domestic and foreign policies. National religious movements as diverse as the Christian Right in the United States and the Taliban in Afghanistan are important factors in the internal politics of particular nations. Moreover, such transnational religious actors as Al-Qaida, Falun Gong, and the Vatican have had important effects on the politics and policies of nations around the world.

Palgrave Studies in Religion, Politics, and Policy serves a growing niche in the discipline of political science. This subfield has proliferated rapidly during the past two decades, and has generated an enormous amount of scholarly studies and journalistic coverage. Five years ago, the journal *Politics and Religion* was created; in addition, works relating to religion and politics have been the subject of many articles in more general academic journals. The number of books and monographs on religion and politics has increased tremendously. In the past, many social scientists dismissed religion as a key variable in politics and government.

This series casts a broad net over the subfield, providing opportunities for scholars at all levels to publish their works with Palgrave. The series publishes monographs in all subfields of political science, including American Politics, Public Policy, Public Law, Comparative Politics, International Relations, and Political Theory.

The principal focus of the series is the public role of religion. "Religion" is construed broadly to include public opinion, religious institutions, and the legal frameworks under which religious politics are practiced. The "dependent variable" in which we are interested is *politics*, defined broadly to include analyses of the public sources and consequences of religious belief and behavior. These would include matters of public policy, as well as variations in the practice of political life. We welcome a diverse range of methodological perspectives, provided that the approaches taken are intellectually rigorous.

The series does not deal with works of theology, in that arguments about the validity or utility of religious beliefs are not a part of the series focus. Similarly, the authors of works about the private or personal consequences of religious belief and behavior, such as personal happiness, mental health, or family dysfunction, should seek other outlets for their writings. Although historical perspectives can often illuminate our understanding of modern political phenomena, our focus in the Religion, Politics, and Policy series is on the relationship between the sacred and the political in contemporary societies.

The Catholic Church in Polish History: Politics, Religion, and Cultural Resistance
By Sabrina P. Ramet

Global Religions and International Relations: A Diplomatic Perspective
By Pasquale Ferrara

Faith-Based Organizations at the United Nations

Jeffrey Haynes

palgrave
macmillan

BL
65
.I55
H38
2014

FAITH-BASED ORGANIZATIONS AT THE UNITED NATIONS
Copyright © Jeffrey Haynes, 2014.

All rights reserved.

First published in 2014 by
PALGRAVE MACMILLAN®
in the United States—a division of St. Martin's Press LLC,
175 Fifth Avenue, New York, NY 10010.

Where this book is distributed in the UK, Europe and the rest of the world,
this is by Palgrave Macmillan, a division of Macmillan Publishers Limited,
registered in England, company number 785998, of Houndmills,
Basingstoke, Hampshire RG21 6XS.

Palgrave Macmillan is the global academic imprint of the above companies
and has companies and representatives throughout the world.

Palgrave® and Macmillan® are registered trademarks in the United States,
the United Kingdom, Europe and other countries.

ISBN: 978-1-137-40915-7

Library of Congress Cataloging-in-Publication Data

Haynes, Jeffrey, 1953–
    Faith-based organizations at the United Nations / by Jeffrey Haynes.
        pages cm. — (Palgrave studies in religion, politics, and policy)
    Includes bibliographical references and index.
    ISBN 978-1-137-40915-7 (hardback)
    1. Religion and international relations. 2. Non-governmental
organizations. 3. United Nations—Decision making. I. Title.

BL65.I55H38 2014
201'.727—dc23   2014026633

A catalogue record of the book is available from the British Library.

Design by Newgen Knowledge Works (P) Ltd., Chennai, India.

First edition: December 2014

10 9 8 7 6 5 4 3 2 1

Contents

CONTENTS

1

Faith-Based Organizations at the United Nations

> Whether liked or disliked, "religious" actors shape governance issues in a global world and awareness of their involvement, value, and contribution is vital for justice, peace, and reconciliation on a wide range of policy issues. *Religious values and concerns inform and shape decision-making and there is much need for more public awareness of the work and significance of religious actors at the UN in achieving (or sometimes subverting) the goals of justice and human rights.* (Emphasis added; Carrette and Miall, 2012: 1)

> Why does international policymaking succeed or fail? What explains the shape that policy takes? Conflict among policy networks is not the only answer to these questions—but it is one important and neglected factor... How does opposition affect international activism and policymaking? (emphasis added; Bob, 2010: 2)

This book examines faith-based organizations (FBOs)[1] and their attempts to influence debate and decision making at the United Nations (UN). The background to this issue is FBOs' growing transnational significance. There is increasing scholarly and policy attention paid to FBOs both in the context of post–Cold War "religious resurgence" and, more generally, "postsecular" international relations. The UN is an important focus of the new postsecular international environment involving FBOs.

The UN is a focal point of global public policy for several reasons. First, it is by far the largest intergovernmental organization (IGO) with 193 member states, where issues of the age are discussed, including human rights, justice, democracy, and development. Second, the UN regularly engages with over 3,500 registered nongovernmental organizations (NGOs), which have consultative status with the UN's Economic and Social Council (ECOSOC), "the United Nations platform on economic and social issues" (http://www.un.org/en/ecosoc/index.shtml). Around 10 percent of NGOs with consultative status with ECOSOC are FBOs. Between 58 percent and 75 percent of the more than 300 FBOs enjoying consultative status with ECOSOC are north-based and Christian. This draws attention to the structure of the UN, where traditionally most power and authority is in the hands of a number of northern (or western) countries, which share a Christian cultural background, including the United States and most member states of the European Union. But given the generally lowly status of faith issues and actors at the UN, the result of the organization's secular-liberal foundations and ethos, what means might FBOs employ seeking to be influential? We shall see that one approach is to be pragmatic—that is, be willing to work with an array of actors, state and non-state, faith-based and secular—in order to try to achieve their objectives. Indeed, as we shall see later, most FBOs at the UN are willing to work with a variety of allies, as long as they share ideological preferences and goals.

Faith-based organizations at the United Nations

Why, how, and with what results do FBOs seek to influence policy formation and dissemination at the UN? Seeking to answer these questions, I present two main arguments in this book: First, the UN has policy-making structures and processes dominated by decision makers seeking to make and implement decisions based on their preferences. Many of the more than 300 FBOs registered at the UN are small- and medium-sized entities, without much in the way of individual financial, diplomatic, or ideological leverage. Consequently, for most FBOs to try to influence UN policy they need to engage in coalition building, working with a range of potential partners, both faith-based and secular. Berger (2003: 10) classifies what she calls "religious NGOs" along a dimension of "pervasiveness" that conceives of religious identity in terms of *degrees* of "religiosity" rather than viewing religious identity as an absolute category. This allows us to conceive of FBOs at the UN as *necessarily* strategic, goal-orientated actors, using a variety of often-pragmatic approaches to try to achieve their goals. The point is that while FBOs are strongly motivated by their faith-based worldviews and values, they still face the same challenges of earthly existence that confront secular non-state actors: securing limited resources and maintaining donor loyalty. In order to compete in an oligopolistic NGO "market" and try and achieve their objectives at the UN, FBOs typically adopt two main strategies: alliance formation and specialization (Hopgood and Vinjamuri, 2012: 38).

Like secular non-state actors, FBOs exhibit much ideological variation at the UN, even when they have roots in a shared faith tradition, such as Christianity or Islam (Barnett and Stein,

2012: 23). For example, socially conservative Catholic FBOs like the Catholic Family and Human Rights Institute have a very different worldview compared to liberal Catholic FBOs, such as Catholics for a Free Choice. Among Muslims, a similar conservative/liberal split can be observed, for example, between the conservative Muslim World League, which has close ideological and financial ties to a powerful Islamic IGO, the Organization of Islamic Cooperation (OIC), and the liberal and autonomous Cairo Institute of Human Rights Studies. Overall, as Berger (2003: 2) notes, FBOs often compete with each other, pushing "for change from both liberal and conservative platforms." In addition, as Petersen (2010) observes, FBOs regularly engage in alliances with secular actors at the UN because they share their liberal or conservative goals. These terms and justification for using them in the book will be explained shortly, but for now it will be enough to note that when examining FBOs at the UN we need to work from the premise that "faith" *per se* is not a fixed or obvious category or value, implying a consistent worldview. For example, many conservative FBOs would probably agree that the UN and its associated liberal *and* secular system encourage development and dissemination of values commensurate with a "secular global order" that by definition conflicts or competes directly with values central to most faith-based understandings (Bob, 2010; 2012). FBOs with liberal values, on the other hand, may well regard the UN as a very important forum to try to counteract conservative faith-based entities, in order to put forward what they see as an appropriate—that is, liberal—faith-based approach. In short, there are big ideological differences between "liberal" and "conservative" FBOs, and it is not correct to presume a general "secular" *versus* "faith" division at the UN between FBOs and secular actors (Berger, 2003: 10).

To date, little focused scholarly or policy-based attention has been paid to FBO activities at the UN, except for a small number of scholars including Berger (2003), Bush (2005), Carrette and Miall, with Beittinger-Lee, Bush, and Trigeaud (2013), Haynes (2013b), and Petersen (2010). This paucity is partly because a significant FBO presence at the UN is a recent phenomenon, having developed only from the 1990s. To a considerable extent, the increased internationalization of FBOs, of which a growing presence at the UN is a key aspect, is the result of new global conditions that have developed over the last quarter century. These include the end of the Cold War in the late 1980s, the dissolution of the Soviet Union in the early 1990s, and the contemporaneous deepening of globalization. The latter significantly facilitated massively increased communications both within and between countries, while enabling FBOs to spread transnationally (Haynes, 2005; 2012; 2013a). The result was that FBOs acquired growing significance in international relations, helping to facilitate what has been called a "cultural turn in world politics." While the UN is said to have had an accommodating attitude to this development, not all has been harmonious, as "religious actors rarely speak with one voice and often target each other." (Kayaoğlu, 2011: 13; also see Kayaoğlu, 2014) A key example of such disharmony was the long-running yet unsuccessful campaign of the OIC, some Islamic FBOs,[2] and several anti-Western governments, including those of China and Russia, to seek to create an international law against "defamation of religion." As we shall see in chapter 6, despite the claim that it was pursuing a universalist measure of value to all faiths, the defamation of religion was perceived by most Western governments, secular NGOs, and some FBOs, to be a self-interested measure motivated by its champions' desire both to deny freedom of expression and, in some cases, to provide further justification to denigrate religious minorities. Kayaoğlu (2011: 13) notes that the main "argument against the measure was that [opponents] believed that the anti-defamation resolution would not only threaten Christian life but also work to block missionaries from prose- lytizing among Muslim-majority nations," and make life (even) harder for religious minorities, such as Ahmadis and *Baha'is*, in some countries (Fox, 2008).

Defamation of religion is perhaps the most egregious extant controversy at the UN involving faith. But it is not the only one. In the book, we examine the role of FBOs, not only in rela- tion to defamation of religion but also in the context of sexual and reproductive health rights (chapter 4) and international development in the context of the Millennium Development Goals (chapter 5). The structure of the book is as follows. The remainder of chapter 1 comprises a number of sections, includ- ing a focus on terminological questions about FBOs, how and why FBOs have developed an important presence at the UN from the 1990s, when there was a series of pivotal conferences involving FBOs and NGOs looking at various topics involv- ing justice and human rights concerns. After that, the chapter looks briefly at the history of the development of the UN, in the context of the general secular trend of international relations from the seventeenth century in order to place today's activi- ties of FBOs at the UN in historical and contemporary context. The rest of this introductory chapter seeks, first, to define FBOs and, second, to explain increased FBO involvement at the UN, which, I contend, can be traced to the ramifications of a series of international conferences on justice and human rights in the 1990s. The overall aim of the introductory chapter is to explain why FBOs have recently gained in importance at the UN, despite that organization's secular-liberal ethos and foundations. Chapter 2 looks at recent and current religious resurgence in the context of postsecular international relations, in order to contextualize the recent increase in numbers of FBOs at the UN. Chapter 3 turns to an examination of the theory and practice of FBOs at the UN. Chapters 4–6 examine three controversial issues involving FBOs at the UN: chapter 4 focuses on sexual and reproductive health rights, chapter 5 on international development in the context of the Millennium Development Goals, and chapter 6 on the tension between human rights and defamation of religion. The final chapter, chapter 7, concludes the book by summarizing its main concerns and suggesting new research questions.

Defining a faith-based organization

What is a FBO? How can the term be defined so as to both clarify its meaning and make it a useful analytical term? We start from the observation that there is no single term in use in the scholarly and policy-related literature that refers to non-state actors influenced by faith. Instead, various terms are used, including: religious NGOs (Berger, 2003); religious international nongovernmental organizations (RINGOs) (Thomas, 2005); religious communities (Banchoff, 2008); religious actors and religious groups (both are used by Kayaoğlu, 2014); faith-based nonprofit organizations (Fitz, n/d); and faith-inspired organizations (Marshall, 2013).

According to Berger (2003: 1), religious NGOs (RNGOs) are

> formal [non-state] organizations whose identity and mission are self-consciously derived from the teachings of one or more religious or spiritual traditions and which operate on a non-profit, independent, voluntary basis to promote and realize collectively articulated ideas about the public good at the national or international level.

In addition, Berger (2003: 1) claims, RNGOs are "characterized by missions rooted in religious and spiritual beliefs," which

> rely on a variety of processes by means of which to reach their goals. Processes such as network building, advocacy, monitoring, and information provision (propaganda) are common to most NGOs while others including spiritual guidance, prayer, and modeling are a unique feature of RNGO operations.

For Petersen (2010: 5), religious NGOs "describe and understand themselves as religious, referring in their name, activities, mission statements or elsewhere to religious traditions, values and ideas." Thomas (2005: 118) builds on these definitions by stressing the transnational nature of a "religious international non-governmental organization" (RINGO). Thomas avers that a RINGO's "mission statement explicitly refers to religious faith as a motivation for its work, its personnel are related to some religious hierarchy or theological tradition, and it hires all or part of its staff on the basis of a creed or statement of faith." In sum, Berger, Petersen, and Thomas all highlight the "religious" *raison d'être* of RNGOs/RINGOs, stressing how they are linked to religious traditions and involve religious personnel. Each of these definitions also shares an assumption that RNGOs and RINGOs are religious counterparts of secular NGOs. Other terms used for broadly similar phenomena—such as, "religious communities" (Banchoff, 2008), "religious actors," and "religious groups" (both Kayaoğlu, 2014)—are more vague, carrying little or no specific analytical meaning.

Some religious studies scholars—for example, Fitzgerald (2012) and Carrette (2013)—insist that "religious" is an incorrect term to use in relation to some important bodies of thought and action, notably Buddhism and Hinduism, which might otherwise be included in the RNGO/RINGO nomenclature.

Fitzgerald (2012: 11) notes that "traditional practices such as yoga or vipassana meditation are normally classified as religious and as parts of the 'religions' Hinduism and Buddhism." Yet, he also reports, such practices are regarded by "experts in yoga and meditation" as "based on empirical observation and experiment. They are in the first place *practices*... [which] share more with the empirical sciences than with Christian faith in the Resurrection, the Virgin Birth, or the Trinitarian God." To use the term "faith" rather than "religion" gets over the problem that Fitzgerald notes—that is, neither Hinduism nor Buddhism are religions in the sense that the term is widely used in relation to the monotheistic Abrahamic religions with their belief in one supreme God. On the other hand, Hinduism, as it is practiced by millions of Indians *is* based on worship of numerous of gods, while many Buddhists, for example, in Burma, Tibet, Sri Lanka, and elsewhere, "worship" Gautama Buddha as virtually or actually a uniquely powerful "god." While in relation to both Hinduism and Buddhism, religion may not be the best term to use for the reasons that Fitzgerald notes, it seems clear that there is a large degree of faith exhibited by millions of Hindus and Buddhists in their worship or very high level of respect shown to deities or "highly exalted figures" in the context of articulation of their spiritual beliefs. For this reason, I will refer to *faith-based* rather than *religious* in this book.

There are a number of terms in use in the scholarly and policy-related literature to refer to non-state actors motivated by faith-linked concerns, including: faith-based nonprofit organization, faith-inspired organization, and faith-based organization. Fitz (n/d) uses the term "faith-based nonprofit organizations" (FNOs) to refer to entities "founded by a religious congregation or religiously-motivated incorporators and board members that clearly states in its name, incorporation, or mission statement that it is a religiously motivated institution." The term FNO has most utility in the United States where recent governments have turned to the faith sector to take over some of the roles and tasks once fulfilled by the state (Haynes, 2008).

Ferris contends that while there "is no generally accepted definition of an FBO," to qualify as an FBO an entity should have the following qualities: affiliation with a religious body; a mission statement with explicit reference to religious values; financial support from religious sources; and/or a governance structure where selection of board members or staff is based on religious beliefs or affiliation; and/or decision-making processes based on religious values. Yet, as Ferris also points out, while such categorizations are theoretically useful, they do have problems, not least because the "variety of faith-based actors makes generalizations difficult" (Ferris, 2005: 312). Not least, she avers, is the problem of potential or actual ideological differences between FBOs that, as we shall see in later chapters, may be as great as those between secular non-state actors and FBOs.

Several authors have also used the term FBO with slight variations in meaning compared to Ferris. For example, Tadros (2010: 7), citing an unidentified United Nations Population Fund source, claims that FBOs have four key characteristics—they are: (1) "faith-based and/or faith-inspired," (2) "inter-faith- or multifaith-based," (3) "local congregations," and (4) "ministries of religious faiths." Wuthnow (2000), on the other hand, characterizes a FBO as having a "religiously-oriented mission statement, support from a religious organization, or being founded by a religious institution" (quoted in Center for Faith and Service, n/d: 2). Both Castelli and McCarthy (1997) and Vidal (2001) divide FBOs into those based on (1) (national) religious congregations; (2) faith-based networks, which might

be national or international denominations, or (3) "freestand-
ing religious organizations, which are incorporated separately
from congregations and national networks." Finally, according
to Vidal (2001: 2), a FBO "is based on a particular ideology
and draws staff, volunteers, or leadership from a particular
religious group." These definitions agree that faith is one of the
key component dimensions of such non-state entities, which
can operate at various levels, including local, national, regional,
and international.

Gerard Clarke (2005) seeks to take things forward definition-
ally by offering a five-point typology of FBOs that, although
focused explicitly on FBOs involved in international development, is also useful more generally. According to Clarke, FBOs
can be:

> *Faith-based representative organizations or apex bodies*, which
> rule on doctrinal matters, govern the faithful and represent
> them through engagement with the state and other actors;
>
> *Faith-based charitable or development organizations*, which
> mobilize the faithful in support of the poor and other social
> groups, and which fund or manage programs that tackle
> poverty and social exclusion;
>
> *Faith-based sociopolitical organizations*, which interpret
> and deploy faith as a political construct, organizing and
> mobilizing social groups on the basis of faith identities but
> in pursuit of broader political objectives or, alternatively,
> promote faith as a sociocultural construct, as a means of
> uniting disparate social groups on the basis of faith-based
> cultural identities;
>
> *Faith-based missionary organizations*, which spread key faith
> messages beyond the faithful, by actively promoting the faith
> and seeking converts to it, or by supporting and engaging
> with other faith communities on the basis of key faith
> principles;
>
> *Faith-based radical, illegal, or terrorist organizations*, which
> promote radical or militant forms of faith identity, engage

in illegal practices on the basis of faith beliefs, or engage in armed struggle or violent acts justified on the grounds of faith.

Clarke's list is a good starting point for identifying what FBOs do and why they do it. On the other hand, it is difficult to understand all FBOs if we accept that they necessarily fall exclusively into one of Clarke's five categories. For example, as Bentyhall (2006) points out, a major Christian development agency, World Vision, seems initially to fit Clarke's category 2—except for the fact that World Vision also raises considerable amounts of money from media campaigns directed toward the general public, which portrays World Vision as a broad-based relief and development agency with its roots firmly in its Christian faith but which also focuses on non-Christian communities, for example, in Palestine (interview with Mae Elise Cannon, World Vision, Washington, DC, January 27, 2012). The International Islamic Relief Organization (IIRO) is another mixed-role FBO that exposes a further problem of Clarke's categorization. IIRO falls into both categories, 2 and 3, emphasizing that many Islamic charities in the Arab world are informally linked to opposition movements, such as the Muslim Brotherhood or al-Qaeda, which falls into category 5. In sum, various definitions of FBOs collectively underline that conceptually to qualify as a FBO such an entity must be clearly connected organizationally, as well as in terms of belief and tradition, with an extant faith community. On the other hand, Holenstein (2006: 81) is correct to suggest that FBOs should not necessarily be regarded as a special and unique category of non-state actor.[3]

In this book, I focus on transnationally focused, faith-based, non-state entities at the UN and there is no consensus about what to call the more than 300 extant examples registered with the ECOSOC. For four reasons, I use the term FBO in this book. First, the use of the term "faith" gets around the problem noted above by Fitzgerald in relation to faith traditions that might cavil at use of the word "religion" to describe them. Second, FBO is almost certainly the most widely used term used in the scholarly and policy literature to refer to various kinds of faith-based, non-state entities. Third, FBO is the term that the UN itself uses (see, for example, a 2013 UN press release from Ban Ki-Moon's office on "The Role of Interfaith Dialogue in Peacebuilding and Women Empowerment," at http://www.un.org/News/Press/docs/2013/sgsm14812.doc.htm).

The fourth reason is that at the UN, some transnational, non-state, faith-based entities akin to "non-secular NGOs" do exist—but they do not form the only category of such actors of analytical significance there. There is also another category of a faith-based, non-state actor active at the UN of an altogether different timbre: transnational, faith-based umbrella entities, unique in international relations, which work at the UN to coordinate actors of various kinds and pursue their faith-linked objectives. The three examples of this kind of actor that I discuss in the book are the Holy See, the World Council of Churches (WCC), and the OIC. Each of these is very active; both Holy See and OIC have Permanent Observer Status in the General Assembly, while the WCC has been closely involved in the workings of the UN since its inception. In addition, each of them is closely involved in campaigns with other kinds of FBOs and secular actors of various kinds, in pursuit of justice and human rights goals in the context of global public policy formation and dissemination at the UN.

The Holy See[4] is both the world's smallest state (1 square kilometer located in the centre of Rome) *and* the focus of the clerical jurisdiction of the Roman Catholic Church. The Holy

See has an important role at the UN, *inter alia*, working with a variety of faith-based and secular state and non-state actors on a human rights agenda, notably in relation to a gender-focused concern with "family values." Its position at the UN is however controversial, including among Roman Catholics. As Bob (2012: 51) notes,

> Since 1964, the Holy See has been a non-member state 'Permanent Observer'—a position unique to any religious organization. In this capacity, it enjoys most rights accorded member states, although it has chosen not to vote on UN resolutions. As such, it is a cornerstone of the religious network, one whose heft rival NGOs cannot match...a leader on 'dignity of the [human] person' issues [at the UN].

The core issue pursued the Holy See at the UN, where it leads a broad-based coalition of like-minded allies, is anti-abortion. "The Holy See underscores the fact that life is a gift from God." Both abortion and euthanasia are

> violation[s] of the Divine Law, an offence against the dignity of the human person, a crime against life and an attempt against humanity to suppress the life of an innocent human being, whether it be fetus or embryo, child or adult, elderly, incurably sick or dying.
>
> (The Holy See, "Abortion Policy," n/d: 2;
> www.un.org/esa/population/publications
> /abortion/doc/holysee.doc)

The Holy See focuses on anti-abortion as a core human rights issue, a concern that helps contour its wider "family values" activities.

The WCC is a 349-member umbrella organization, a "global fellowship of churches" ("An Introduction to the World Council of Churches," n/d: p.3). *The WCC seeks "visible church unity" and is concerned with the collective interests of non-Roman Catholic Christians.*

The WCC is the broadest and most inclusive among many organized expressions of the modern ecumenical movement, which seeks visible church unity. The fellowship includes most of the world's Orthodox churches, the Old Catholic and Mar Thoma churches, churches of the historic denominational traditions such as the Anglican, Baptist, Lutheran, Methodist, and Reformed, many united and uniting churches as well as churches such as the Mennonite, Friends, Congregational, and Disciples.

("An Introduction to the World Council of Churches," n/d: p.3)

The WCC is most concerned with "justice" and uses its position at the UN as a way of focusing and directing its Christian concerns to seek better development outcomes for the world's poorest people. In this context, the WCC is highly critical of the current globalization that it believes is polarizing the rich and the poor (World Council of Churches, 2001).

The OIC "is the second largest intergovernmental organization after the United Nations," with 57 "member states spread over four continents." The OIC seeks to be "the collective voice of the Muslim world," aiming to "safeguard and protect the interests of the Muslim world in the spirit of promoting international peace and harmony among various people of the world." (http://www.oic-oci.org/oicv2/page/?p_id=52&p_ref=26&lan=en). Like the Holy See, the OIC is very unusual in international relations: a faith-based entity that brings together both states and non-states under an umbrella campaigning organization whose remit is, on the one hand, to advance the interests of a faith community and, on the other, pursue wider justice and human rights goals that transcend the interest of just one faith. In sum, the Holy See, the WCC, and the OIC are important focal points of faith-based activity at the UN, using their abilities to pursue justice and human rights goals on behalf of both their faith constituencies and a wider international community. We look at the Holy See (and Roman Catholic Church more generally) in chapter 4, which is concerned with sexual and reproductive health rights. The WCC's fractious relationship with the World Bank is examined in chapter 5, concerned with human development in the context of the Millennium Development Goals. Chapter 6 is concerned with the defamation of religion controversy, which centrally engaged the attention of the OIC. Finally, the case studies in chapters 4–6 highlight that FBOs at the UN are engaged in justice and human rights concerns that transcend "narrow" faith issues and whose activities involve coalitions of faith-based and secular actors, both state and non-state.

United Nations conferences on justice and human rights in the 1990s: the role of FBOs

FBOs are often examined in local and/or national contexts. Only recently has the analysis extended to include international and transnational settings. A small but growing number of scholars—including, Berger (2003), Boehle (2010), Doebbler (2013), Dogan (2005), Haynes (2001; 2012; 2013a; 2013b; 2014), Kayaoğlu (2011; 2014), Knox (2002), Leaustean (2013), and Petersen (2010)—have begun to examine international or transnational FBO activities, often with a focus on, *inter alia*, the European Union (Leaustean, Haynes), the Organization of Islamic Cooperation (Doebbler, Dogan, Haynes), or the United Nations (Berger, Boehle, Haynes, Kayaoğlu, Knox, and Petersen).

In regard to the UN, Knox (2002: 5) traces the beginning of the increased involvement of FBOs from the early 1990s. Generally, this was a time of increasing global public policy concerns, following the end of the Cold War and the contemporaneous expansion and deepening of globalization (Haynes, 2005, 2013a; Haynes et al., 2011). These concerns stimulated a series of international UN conferences on how to improve justice and human rights. The topics were human rights (Vienna, 1992), the natural environment (Rio de Janeiro, 1992), population growth (Cairo, 1994), human development (Copenhagen, 1995), women and gender (Beijing, 1995), and social development (Geneva, 2000). These conferences collectively provided crucial focal points and encouragement for many FBOs, previously focused on local or national issues, to extend their activities to the UN, widely seen as a crucial generator of global public policy (Bob, 2012).

Reflecting this, numbers of FBOs registered with ECOSOC at the UN have recently grown rapidly. In 2002, a "Religion Counts" report, "Religion and Public Policy at the UN," identified 180 out of 2000 NGOs at the UN as religious—that is, 9 percent. In 2003, Berger (2003) identified 263 FBOs, that is, 8.77 percent of the then 3,000 NGOs linked to the ECOSOC. In 2008, Petersen (2010) found that 320 NGOs at the UN registered with ECOSOC were religious out of a total of 3,183 (10.05%). Thus, over a decade, numbers of FBOs registered with ECOSOC nearly doubled from 180 to 320, although in percentage terms the ratio with secular NGOs has remained constant at around 9 percent. Note, however, that this number does not include the Holy See, the WCC, or the OIC, whose influence and coordinating activities are individually and collectively significant.

Carrette and Miall (2012: 10) note that "there has been a significant increase in the number of NGOs in consultation with the UN since the 1990s, but little is known about the place of 'religion' in this network." What is however known is that most FBOs active at the UN are both north-based and Christian (Petersen, 2010). Jewish FBOs are also relatively well represented. Other faiths—including, Islam, Hinduism, and Buddhism—are significantly underrepresented at the UN, as are south-based FBOs more generally. Overrepresentation of north-based, Christian FBOs can be ascertained from the current ECOSOC list of more than 3,700 registered NGOs.[5] Examining the list of registered NGOs in 2008—when 3,183 such entities were listed—Petersen (2010) identified 320 (10.05%) as religious or, in the terminology of this book, faith-based. This number included: 187 Christian (58%), 52 Islamic (16%), 25 generically "spiritual" (8%), 22 Jewish (7%), 14 Buddhist (4%), 11 "multi-religious" (3%), six "others" (2%), and three Hindu (1%).

During a major research project over three years (2010–2012) focusing on FBOs at the UN,[6] Carrette and Miall (2012) found that 75 percent of FBOs registered with ECOSOC are Christian and north-based—that is, they located in North America or western Europe. Many among them are both well organized and influential, often both those with the UN and those with individual governments are wealthy; some are extremely wealthy. Such an observation is not new. In 2001, Berger (2003) noted, three US-based Christian FBOs—the Salvation Army, World Vision, and Catholic Relief Services—had combined annual revenues of over US$1.6 billion. More than 150 million people were involved in their international and transnational FBO networks (Berger 2003: 2). In 2011, World Vision's annual income was "approaching $3 billion" (Hopgood and Vinjamuri, 2012: 37), while that of the Salvation Army was US$2.83 bn. (http://www.forbes.com/companies/salvation-army/). Catholic Relief Services' income lagged behind the other two, although in 2010 it still amounted to US$918 million (http://crs.org/about/finance/pdf/AR_2010.pdf).

Thus, over a decade (2001–2011) the combined income of these three US-based Christian FBOs more than quadrupled: from $1.6 bn. to around $6.75 bn. The massive growth in income was not however the only key asset that such entities enjoyed. Their income and hugely influential networks enabled them to exploit UN arrangements and norms both organizationally and ideologically to increase their advantage and leverage. According to Carrette and Miall (2012), this is linked to the fact that both "formation and structure of the UN [are] shaped by the Judaic-Christian heritage which constituted the modern forms of international politics, including the notions of sovereignty, secularism, civil society and individual belief." Berger (2003: 17) concurs, asserting that

> it is possible that involvement with the UN and NGO creation is compatible with Christian culture and ideology, given the involvement of churches in the formative process of the UN (e.g. World Council of Churches), their desire to influence the secular polity and their access to material resources.

Many north-based Christian FBOs at the UN are, for example, active at the Human Rights Council helping shape protocols on various issues, including child soldiers, the rights of women, and the condition of prisoners in goal. Yet, to be influential at the UN, FBOs do not "just" need to have significant financial resources and networks of supporters and followers. It also helps greatly to have major and sustained commitment and appropriate specialist expertise as well as ability to build and maintain support of both governments in order to make sustained progress on human rights issues. This is not to say that all FBOs are equal in their abilities in these regards. As Carrette and Miall (2012) explain,

> there are significant differences in funding and access to diplomats between NGO groups...Religious NGOs at the UN

in New York are involved at all levels of activity in initiating issues, advocacy, network and representation on UN committees...Religious actors depend on the support of states for actions that support awareness of religion and its significance to peace and security

This highlights the potentially pivotal role that influential umbrella organizations, such the Holy See, the WCC, and the OIC, can play in accessing diplomats and networks in pursuit of their objectives. In sum, for FBOs to progress their objectives at the UN it helps to be rich, organizationally astute, and savvy about how to achieve goals, while demonstrating willingness to work with various entities, including other FBOs, secular NGOs, and governments. Often, north-based Christian FBOs have more of the necessary assets in these regards, compared to other types of FBOs. However, the influential position of north-based Christian FBOs at the UN does not reflect current demographic realities of Christianity, which is now increasingly a south-based faith. Today, more than half the world's Christians live in three developing regions (Asia Pacific, Latin America, and Sub-Saharan Africa), while numbers of north-based Christians—mainly in North America and Europe—have declined. This is part of a long-term demographic trend: between 1910 and 2010, the global proportion of Christians living in Europe fell from two-thirds (66.3%) to one-quarter (25.9%) (Pew Forum, 2011). During the same time, the percentage of Christians living in the Americas grew from 27.1 percent to 36.8 percent although this was mainly due to growth of Christianity in Latin America rather than North America (Csillag, 2013).

Apart from the issue of where Christians live, it is also the case that Christian FBOs registered with ECOSOC are overrepresented at the UN in relation to overall numbers of Christians.

Globally, there were approximately 2.18 bn. Christians in 2010 (Pew Forum, 2011) and about 1.65 bn. Muslims. As there were then around seven billion people (7.067 billion), we might anticipate that Christians (30.8%) and Muslims (23.3%) would have similar percentages of FBOs at the UN. Yet, as already noted, Petersen (2010) identified 58 percent of FBOs at the UN as Christian, while Carrette and Miall's recent (2012) survey identified 75 percent of UN FBOs as *both* Christian *and* north-based. Islamic FBOs amount to only one-sixth of ECOSOC-registered FBOs at the UN. Thus, Christians (30.8% of people in the world) are "overrepresented" at the UN (as Christian FBOs are between 58 and 75 percent of total ECOSOC-registered FBOs at the UN). Muslims (23.3%) are significantly "underrepresented," with just 16 percent of ECOSOC-registered FBOs at the UN. In addition, in 2012 there were an estimated 13.76 million Jews in the world, less than 2 percent of the global population, whereas Jewish FBOs accounted for 7 percent of the total number of ECOSOC-registered FBOs at the UN; thus, Jews too are overrepresented at the UN compared to their global numbers, while, not only Muslims, but also Hindus (14% of global population/2% of ECOSOC-registered FBOs) and Buddhists (7%/4%), are significantly underrepresented.

In 2008, there were 52 Islamic, 22 Jewish, 14 Buddhist, and 3 Hindu FBOs registered with ECOSOC. As Petersen (2010) notes, FBOs "are often motivated by conceptions of a divine justice and man's duty to work for the realization of this." This is not to say that all FBOs from whatever faith tradition see a similar appropriateness in embarking on politicized campaigns at the UN or anywhere else. While many Christian FBOs seem to find it easy to make the link between "divine justice and man's duty to work for the realization of this," most Buddhist, Hindu, and Jewish FBOs do not. That is, while they may mention their religious values and ideas in their mission statements, this does not imply that they are willing to pursue their goals via politicized channels at the UN or elsewhere. Many Islamic FBOs refer to quotes from the Qur'an as well as sayings and stories of the Prophet Mohammed, expressing the religious duty to help people in need. For example, Islamic Relief UK's website contains a quotation from the Qur'an: "Whoever saved a life, it would be as if they saved the life of all mankind" (Qur'an 5:32). As well as seeking to respond to "disasters and emergencies," Islamic Relief UK "promotes sustainable economic and social development by working with local communities—regardless of race, religion or gender." (http://www.islamic-relief.org.uk/about-us/). Most Jewish FBOs, on the other hand, have a different *modus vivendi*. Most were created in the first half of the twentieth century, for a specific purpose: to pursue the goal of a homeland for the Jews, which came into reality with the UN-backed foundation of the state of Israel in 1948. Today, however, Jewish FBOs have a varied relationship with the government of that state.

> While some Jewish NGOs are ambivalent in their relation to the Israeli state and its politics, most do seem to express some degree of sympathy, formulated partly as a support to the country's Palestine policy, partly as a critique of the UN treatment of Israel. Even the most progressive Jewish NGOs do not directly oppose or criticize the Israeli state. However, primarily conservative NGOs have entered into cooperation with Israel,
>
> (Petersen, 2010)

Finally, the handful of Buddhist and Hindu FBOs at the UN, such as the World Fellowship of Buddhists, the Asian Buddhist Conference for Peace and the Hindu Council of New Zealand, are chiefly active in interfaith dialogue and development contexts.

While hundreds of (mainly north-based Christian) FBOs are entitled to be interlocutors with officials and policy makers at the UN via their institutionalized status afforded by ECOSOC-registration, this does not necessarily imply that they are able to exert influence consistently on global public policy debates. Trying to exert such influence is especially problematic when FBOs try and act alone, employing solely religious arguments. To acquire and exercise influence at the UN necessitates that FBOs seek partners and allies, including other FBOs, secular NGOs, and states. Why should such entities ally themselves with FBOs to try to influence policy debates at the UN? Such alliances occur, according to Bob (2012), in pursuit of shared ideological goals. In other words, various entities—both secular and religious ones—work together because they share goals, not necessarily out of shared religious convictions, but as a result of shared ideological principles and beliefs. On their own, most FBOs struggle at the UN to be taken seriously, with no automatic right to be heard in global policy debates; in this context, seeking allies to pursue goals is crucial. In addition, FBOs must learn to adapt to UN norms and conventions, in order to be heard and accepted. This means that to be significant players in global public policy debates, they must necessarily adopt and adapt to the terms and rationale of liberal—that is, nonreligious—discourse, *even when they do not agree with it.* As we shall later, this is precisely what key FBO umbrella entities, including the Holy See, WCC, and OIC, do in order to try to maximize influence and leverage

However, according to Kayaoğlu (2011: 2), "adoption of liberal discourse by religious groups" at the UN makes Muslims "vulnerable as liberals set the parameters of their discourse." This highlights, more generally, how Muslims are in a difficult position at the UN and other international fora. In particular after September 11, 2001, Muslims are widely perceived in the West as linked to illiberal and authoritarian views. In addition, as Kayaoğlu notes, we can see an intellectually dominant "Habermasian postsecularism" (Habermas, 2007), which, characterized by a nonreligious liberalism, serves to "marginalize Islamic discourse in the (international) public sphere" (ibid.).

Where is faith at the UN?

Kayaoğlu is identifying an important issue here, of direct relevance to the concerns of this book: How and why do FBOs interact with each other and with secular actors at the UN, and with what results? To what extent are FBOs willing to "sign up" to the UN's liberal and secular values, in order to gain entry into debates and discussions at the UN? The point is that to be seen and heard at the UN, FBOs *must* accord with the organization's secular, liberal, and irreligious values, norms, and beliefs, and this is obviously a problem for entities whose very *raison d'être* is faith-based values, norms, and related goals. This reminds us that when assessing the impact of FBOs at the UN, it is important to bear in mind that the UN is a demonstrably secular organization, founded on nonreligious values, which underpin and reflect the characteristics and global spread of a post-Westphalian, West-directed and focused international order (Haynes, Hough, Malik, and Pettiford, 2011). In addition, three specific structural characteristics of international relations encourage the involvement at the UN of north-based Christian FBOs, and serve to undermine the likelihood of other FBOs making their mark there: (1) "The international political system is a development of the Judaeo-Christian beliefs," (2) The UN's modus operandi favors certain types of religion and religious NGOs, and (3) "There is a convention [at the UN]

not to talk about religion, and not to talk in religious terms"
(Carrette and Miall, 2012).

The secular character and philosophy of the UN is an ideational choice, whose adoption stems from the founding of the
UN in 1945, an era of international relations where faith-based
values were not an important or overt aspect of the norms and
values underpinning the emergence of a more cooperative world
order following World War II. The secular foundations of the
UN were still apparent more than six decades later. Evidence
for this comes from a 2008 conversation at the UN, reported
by Hurd (2011: 1), between two Harvard University professors:
Father Bryan Hehir, a Catholic priest and secretary for Health
Care and Social Services in the Archdiocese of Boston, and John
Gerard Ruggie, at the time special representative of the UN
secretary general for Business and Human Rights.[7] According
to Hurd, Hehir said to Ruggie: "Where is religion at the UN?"
and Ruggie replied: "There is none." On the face of it, Ruggie's
reply is puzzling, given the fact that the UN is a focal point for
hundreds of FBOs, including highly important FBO umbrella
groups (including, the Holy See, the OIC, the WCC) and various
influential states, including Iran and Saudi Arabia, whose state
policy is officially faith-based. It is perhaps only possible to make
sense of Ruggie's comments when we see them in the context
of the UN's foundational secular and liberal institutions and
associated ideational framework, which denies, albeit implicitly,
any formal or institutionalized role for faith. This is made clear
in the following quotations from two senior UN employees, Ban
Ki-Moon, UN secretary general, and Azza Karam, senior advisor
on Culture at the United Nations Population Fund (UNFPA).

> As a secular organization, the United Nations has no common
> religion. But, like all the major faiths, we too work on behalf of
> the disadvantaged and the vulnerable...I have long believed

that when governments and civil society work toward a common goal, transformational change is possible. Faiths and religions are a central part of that equation

> (emphasis added; Ban Ki-moon, November 3, 2009)
> http://www.un.org/News/Press/docs/2009
> /sgsm12585.doc.htm

Assessing partnerships between UN Agencies and FBOs was one of the primary goals of the consultations. The kinds of challenges underlying such partnerships had been addressed before by UN staff at the UN Inter-Agency Consultation on FBO Engagement, held at UNFPA headquarters on July 9, 2008. During those proceedings, UN agency representatives noted the following challenges: '*Unease in engaging religion within the United Nations system.*'

> (emphasis added; Karam, 2012: 19)

In the first quotation, Ban Ki-moon refers to what is historically a key focus of the United Nations: its worldview as a "secular organization." Today, however, and the second part of his quotation points to this, the UN, in seeking to diminish and ultimately do away with gross disparities by improving "development" outcomes, especially among the world's poorest people and countries, now claims to takes faith-based civil society actors seriously. This should be understood in the context of the UN's primary objective: building greater collective security, where deepening developmental polarization between rich and poor is understood to be a major global driver of intensifying conflict and insecurity. This concern was a driving force behind the UN's current collective initiative in relation to improving international development outcomes: the Millennium Development Goals (MDGs) (2000–2015). As we shall see in chapter 4, the MDGs are noteworthy, not least because of FBOs' significant and novel involvement, including that of the WCC. More generally, the MDGs represented, for the first time, significant collective involvement of both state and non-state actors, secular and faith-based, in seeking to plan, prioritize, and deliver wide-ranging international development aspirations and goals. This contrasts with a few years ago when FBOs were regarded with suspicion—or worse—by most secular development actors (Haynes, 2007; 2013b).

In the second quotation, Azza Karam highlights a key factor when seeking to understand and assess the role today of religion at the UN: "Unease in engaging religion within the United Nations system." Despite its secular foundations, ethos, and focus, today the UN finds itself regularly grappling with various moral and ethical issues, including justice and human rights issues, which frequently overlap with FBO concerns. This has come about in the context of changing concerns in global public policy, a key factor facilitating growing significance of faith-based issues at the UN. Today hundreds of FBOs have the right to engage with the UN via ECOSOC registration and, as long as they ostensibly and consistently adhere to UN values,[8] they are able to act at the UN as credible—albeit sometimes controversial—interlocutors on various moral and ethical issues. As we shall see in later chapters, these concerns include sexual and reproductive health rights, international development, and defamation of religion. This emphasizes that, contrary to what Ruggie avers, there are numerous issues at the UN, which FBOs believe they have a right to try to influence, whether working alone or, more likely, engaging with a variety of state and non-based actors, both secular and faith-based.

Conclusion

"The United Nations is first and foremost an intergovernmental body that owes its existence and is accountable to its 192 (sic) member states"[9] (Karam (2012: 23). This implies that the UN's primary reference point is the collective grouping of world governments, coming together in the UN General Assembly. This structure of governance was created primarily to give credence to the UN's overarching human rights mandate and today provides the context to and explains the ways that the UN provides support to both governments and civil society actors. In order to comprehend why faith-based actors are now taken seriously at the UN, we need briefly to examine the UN's development over time. We also need to take account of the impact of a "widespread religious resurgence" in what is sometimes referred to as postsecular international environment. These topics inform the subject matter of the next chapter.

2

Religious Resurgence and Postsecular International Relations

> We can only make sense of the burgeoning interest in the nexus between religion and [the UN], if we *historicize* it within the context of what has generally come to be understood as the turn to the postsecular in the social world and scholarly enquiry. (Habermas, 2006, quoted in Bettiza, 2013: 13)

Increasing numbers of FBOs at the UN coincide with both a general resurgence of religion and postsecular international relations. Both developments have occurred over the last 25 years, following the end of the Cold War, the dissolution of the Soviet Union, and the deepening and widening of globalization. What are the characteristics and dimensions of a general resurgence of religion and of postsecular international relations? To what extent, if at all, is international relations today characterized by a "renewed openness to questions of the spirit" leading to a "renewed interest in the spiritual life," said to characterize the postsecular? Finally, do burgeoning FBO numbers enable us to conclude that there is a new emphasis and focus on the postsecular in global public policy at the UN?

Before seeking to answer these questions, it is useful to start the chapter with descriptions of and explanations for both the onset of postsecular international relations and, more generally, recent and continuing resurgence of religion, which some see as a global phenomenon. Both developments come in the context of declining membership of organized religions and apparently inexorable advance of growth of secularization in some regions, notably western Europe (Norris and Inglehart, 2004). This chapter is structured in the following way. The first section seeks to define and understand what the terms "secular" and "postsecular" imply for our understanding of FBOs at the UN. Section two looks at the analytical implications of the return of faith to international relations. The third section examines the evolution of the UN, as a secular organization in a world increasingly characterized by the significance of postsecularity.

Defining and understanding the secular and the postsecular

Secularism, the state or quality of being *secular*, the end result of a process of secularization, is a term that was for decades associated in Western social science, including international relations, with terms like "worldly" and "temporal." Secular implied a lack of reference to a transcendent order, that is, one involving a divine being or beings, such as God or gods. The notion of secularism became normatively associated both with universalist pretensions—that is, it would become a global phenomenon—and a claim to superiority over each and every set of religious ideas, irrespective of their origin, content, philosophy, or approach. After World War II, secularism became an ideology of domination, implying marginalization, downgrading and, in some cases, belittling of religious ideas, sacrificed in pursuit of "rationality," "progress," and "modernity." Over time, the domain of the secular became strongly associated with normatively desirable attributes, such as, tolerance, common sense, justice, rational argument, public interest, and public authority. Religion was pejoratively regarded as the antithesis of secularism (Hurd, 2008).

Postsecular is used in a variety of ways in the social sciences literature. Nynas and Pessi (2012: 163) understand it to refer to "*complex and diverse changes that in different ways involve*, among others, *resacralization¹or revitalization of religion*." For international relations (IR) scholars, the postsecular poses a dual challenge: (1) seeking to understand how resurgence of faith poses both theoretical and methodological challenges to IR, a very secular discipline, and (2) trying to comprehend empirically what characterizes postsecular international relations.

In recent years, there have been attempts to conceptualize the postsecular in international relations to take into account religious resurgence. While Charles Taylor (2007) has recently examined secularism at length, Jürgen Habermas (2006) has sought to examine a *post*secularism in western Europe. For Habermas, the interesting question is why some apparently secularized societies in western Europe have moved toward a postsecular condition. For Habermas, such societies, including for example, the United Kingdom (UK), Germany, and the Netherlands, exhibit renewed social and political importance for some faith entities—including traditionally powerful churches, for example, the Church of England in the United Kingdom and "new" religious communities, notably

Muslims—who, in order to defend their interests, seek greater public voice, relevance, and significance.

Habermas notes that today's postsecular societies must at some stage have been secular. This is because logically, the controversial term postsecular can only be applied to once secular societies in western Europe, as well as countries such as Canada, Australia, and New Zealand, whose development coincided with their domination by western European settlers and which also exhibit today pronounced secular characteristics. Over time, in these countries, popular religious ties have steadily lapsed, sometimes dramatically, in recent decades (Norris and Inglehart, 2004). The great majority of citizens are secular and, as a result, they inhabit a secularized society, that is, a society made secular over time as a result of a process of secularization.

Habermas (2006) also notes that in terms of sociological indicators, there is no widespread return to religious behavior and convictions among most local populations in western Europe. Trends toward de-institutionalized and new spiritual forms of religiosity have not offset tangible losses by major traditional religious communities, especially Christian churches. According to Habermas, three overlapping phenomena now converge to create the impression of a widespread resurgence of religion: an expansion in missionary activities; a widespread "fundamentalist" radicalization that has affected all world religions (i.e., Buddhism, Christianity, Hinduism, Islam, and Judaism); and, finally, an increased instrumentalization of the political potential for violence said to be innate in all five world faiths. In conclusion, for Habermas the postsecular is characterized by resurgence of religion with baleful impacts on stability and security as a result of a corresponding growth in religion-related violence and extremism.

The issues that Habermas raises are of relevance beyond western Europe to include wider concerns in international relations, including the role and characteristics of FBOs at the UN and what it means for our understanding of what they do when we talk of the postsecular. It raises two important questions:

▸ How can a focus on postsecularity inform debates and understandings about important current issues at the UN in relation to core concerns of justice and human rights?
▸ What are the implications of these debates on the postsecular for thinking about international relations and global politics, including in relation to FBOs at the UN?

Such questions, although not necessarily easy to answer, are of major importance for our understanding of current international relations. It is crucial to engage with them, if we want to engage meaningfully with current international relations and the extent to which it is informed today by faith concerns. The questions are of special relevance when thinking about what many would agree is the most important body of actors in today's international relations consistently informed by faith issues: transnational FBOs, including the more than 300 registered with the Economic and Social Council of the UN or the 180 in regular interaction with the European Union (Haynes, 2013c; 2014).

More generally, a focus on transnational FBOs is important within the context of post–Cold War globalization. This is often said to be a pivotal factor encouraging FBOs to involve themselves in cross-border issues, often focusing attention on national, regional, or international governance frameworks (Thomas, 2005; Haynes, 2007; Leustean, 2013). This is because globalization greatly facilitates increased links between state and non-state actors, both faith-based and secular, in a novel context where neither geographical distance nor international borders are any longer insuperable barriers to regular or routine communications. As Peter Beyer (1994: 1) notes: "We now live in a globalizing social reality, one in which previously effective barriers to communication no longer exist." Globalization theoretically increases the ability of cross-border networks, both secular and faith-based, to disseminate information and ideas and to link up with like-minded groups across international borders. In addition, over the past two decades or so, global migration patterns have also helped spawn more active religious transnational communities (Cesari, 2010; Levitt, 2004). The overall result is that cross-border links involving religious entities have multiplied, and, in many cases, so have their justice and human rights concerns and foci (Haynes, 2012; Shah, Stepan, and Toft, 2012; Thomas, 2005). In short, according to Banchoff (2008), globalization leads to more active religious transnational communities, creating a powerful force in international relations.

Over time, states are often said to be losing their preeminent position in international relations, challenged by an array of important transnational non-state actors, especially those with financial and/or diplomatic clout. Examples include: transnational business corporations; international financial institutions, especially the World Bank, International Monetary Fund, and World Trade Organization; regional intergovernmental organizations, such as the European Union and the North American Free Trade Agreement; and multiregion FBOs, such as the Organization of Islamic Cooperation, the Roman Catholic Church, and the World Council of Churches. In widely cited contributions, Susanne Hoeber Rudolph (1997; 2005) claims that today we are witnessing the de facto "fading of the state," providing unique opportunities for FBOs to expand their activities and influence. Rudolph sees this as particularly important in the context of a rapidly burgeoning "transnational civil society," which, she avers, offers the chance to develop a global, "poly-faith" "ecumene." Put another way, assuming that forms of polity and institutionalized expressions of faith via FBOs have an effect on each other, we can hypothesize that Rudolph's claimed state "thinning" and linked "porousness" of interstate boundaries, as a result of globalization and consequential expansion of transnational political, social, and economic institutions and epistemes,[2] significantly affects both forms of faith and the capacity to achieve faith-linked goals in international relations, including via interactions at the UN.

Toft, Philpott, and Shah point to the importance of globalization for the expanding influence of FBOs. They argue that this is made possible by massive advances in

> modern communication and transportation... [which have] propelled one of the most striking dimensions of the [religious] resurgence—*the evolution of religious communities into transnational political actors.* The Muslim Brotherhood spans multiple countries and communicates its ideas globally. Hindu nationalists in India are supported by equally ardent Hindus in the United States. National Catholic churches around the world were supported by the Vatican—though to different degrees—in their confrontations against dictatorships. *Religious communities have spilled over the confines not only of the private and the local but also over the borders of the sovereign state.* (emphases added; 2011: 14–15)

Note that Toft, Philpott, and Shah are referring to complex, multidimensional FBOs, including the Muslim Brotherhood, transnational Hindu nationalist networks, and complex transnational Catholic entities. Such international actors have been of major significance since the end of the Cold War and their influence is a key component of a wider return or resurgence of faith in international relations.

The "return" of faith to international relations

The term postsecular is now widely used in various academic disciplines, including sociology, political science, political philosophy, theology, history, and, increasingly, IR. Sociologists understand postsecular in the context of a (generally) unexpected return of religion into previously secularized societies. In this view, the postsecular is characterized by new visibility of religious practices and religious attitudes in previously secular public spaces, including those in western Europe, previously believed to be inexorably secularizing. For political scientists, evidence of postsecularity is to be found in the necessity of reevaluating how governments engage with religion and adapting their policies to requirements of increasingly religiously pluralist societies in, for example, western Europe, long regarded as moving inexorably along the path of secularization. In addition, there is the issue of religious freedom and the role of religious actors in the public sphere in western Europe's increasingly multicultural national environments. Political philosophers view "postsecularity" as a normative challenge that, on the one hand, defines the place of religious viewpoints in the democratic public sphere and, on the other, serves to formulate a political ethic with general validity among citizens, irrespective of which faith—if any—they belong to. Philosophers address questions about the relevance of religiously informed arguments in morality and ethics debates, including those to do with gender equality, women's right and access to abortion services, and the scourge of HIV/AIDS and how to deal with the pandemic. Theologians tend to examine postsecularity as a condition within which Christian churches and other institutionalized religious identities strive to find both place and role in relation to the state and civil society, which are no solely longer determined—at least in western Europe—by exclusively secularist criteria. Finally, historians place postsecularity in the broader historical context of modernization and cultural history, aiming to identify specific historical processes and conditions that led to secularization and now, perhaps, lead out of it.

The varied and various ideas expressed by sociologists, political scientists, political philosophers, philosophers, theologians, and historians to include the postsecular suggests that the term is not static or its meaning agreed; it means different things to different people in different contexts. That is, postsecular does not have clear and consistent meaning in any of these disciplinary contexts. Yet, there are also discernible commonalities. There is a shared understanding that the relationship between religion and politics, society, philosophy, and so on, is in need of reconceptualization in the light of a continued—or renewed or increasing—religious presence, even in societies—such as those in western Europe, once almost unanimously believed to be inexorably secularizing—as a crucial aspect of the perceived linear trajectory from tradition to modernity. One way of thinking of this idea of religious resurgence and factoring it into an analysis of international relations—along with political science, perhaps the most secular of all of the social sciences— is to go for the lowest common denominator that runs through the various definitions provided in the paragraph above. There, postsecular refers in essence to a "renewed openness to questions of the spirit" (King, 2000), with a postsecular society identified by Dalferth (2010) as one with new or "renewed interest in the spiritual life."

What does this mean for our understanding of international relations? First, we need to remind ourselves that international relations was, for hundreds of years, conventionally secular—increasingly since the Peace of Westphalia (1648) that ended Europe's decades-long inter-Christian (Protestants and Catholics) conflict. What does it mean for our understanding of international relations to make the claim that we now inhabit a postsecular global environment? According to Geoghegan,

> secularism is a complex and multifaceted process which emerged out of the European wars of religion in the sixteenth century, postsecularism is a heuristic and political device to address aspects of that process. *Postsecularism is a contested concept that lends itself to ambiguity.* It could suggest a deeply antagonistic stance toward secularism, involving the call for a resurgent religiosity, where "post" really implies "pre"—a *dismantling of the secular culture of the past few centuries* (emphasis added; Geoghegan, 2000: 205–206)

To focus on these issues, it is useful to start by identifying what postsecular might mean in international relations, so we can seek to operationalize it analytically.

> ▸ Does the small, yet arguably growing influence of religious entities in some states' foreign policies indicate that IR more generally is now characterized by postsecularity?
>
> ▸ Is there persuasive evidence of a shift in IR from the dominance of secular concerns to a situation where religious actors of various kinds are now consistently able to influence outcomes?

The return of religion[3] to international relations and the turn to what is often referred to as a postsecular international context is often understood as a historically recent phenomenon. It has occurred following decades of apparently relentless secularization that, accorded its own theory, became a virtual law of the social sciences in the first seven decades of the twentieth century. The return of religion in the 1980s, following Iran's Islamist revolution, defied conventional social scientific wisdom. Until that time, most (Western) social scientists agreed that secularization theory significantly captured the reality and trajectory of universal human development, a one-way process whereby religion would *inevitably* and *everywhere* lose its hegemonic public position to fade into irrelevance. Following the Peace of Westphalia in 1648, relentless secularization was matched in international relations thinking by creation and development of emphatically secular global organizational structures and processes during the twentieth century with the League of Nations followed by the United Nations (Bellin, 2008; Haynes, 2013a; Philpott, 2009; Snyder, 2011). This reflected the fact that, during the twentieth century, it became conventional wisdom among Western social scientists that, linked to the hegemonic theories of modernization and political development, the future of well-integrated nation-states lay everywhere in secular participatory politics. In order successfully to build nation-states, political leaders needed to remain as neutral as possible from entanglements of particularistic—especially faith-based and ethnicity-related—political claims. As a result, politics had to be separated from such claims in order to avoid dogmatism and to encourage citizens' tolerance, within which context democracy might have a chance to flourish. As decades of apparently unstoppable movement toward increasingly secular societies in Western and other "modernized" parts of the world underlined, both faith and piety became ever more private matters. Over time, faith was relegated to the category of a (minor) problem that should not be allowed to intrude into the universal search for both national unity and political stability and development based on democracy. The consequence was that, for decades until the 1970s, secularization theory was hegemonic in exhibiting a key social scientific assumption: as societies modernize they secularize and when they secularize faith-based concerns lose most or even all of their former public salience.

Things changed significantly in this regard following the end of the Cold War in the late 1980s, the subsequent dissolution of the Soviet Union a few years later, and the increased impact of globalization. Together, these three conceptually distinct yet in practice related developments emphasized that politics, economics, and human interactions do not end at the water's edge. Reflecting this changed environment and associated expanded non-state actor involvement in international relations, the last 20 years have seen significant and sustained growth in extra-national political entities, including a huge number of transnational non-state entities, including FBOs. In 2000, there were an estimated 26,000 "international NGOs" (INGOs), up from an estimated 6,000 in 1990 (Ferris, 2005: 312). By 2014, there were an estimated 40,000 INGOs (http://www.ngo.in/), a seven-fold increase in 25 years. At the UN, as already noted, ECOSOC registers more than 3,700 INGOs, around one-tenth of the global total. Of that number, around 10 percent are reckoned to be FBOs (Petersen, 2010: 5; Carrette and Miall, 2013).

Petersen estimated that the 2008 total of 3,183 INGOs registered at the UN included 320 (10.05%), which she identified as "spiritual" or "religious." As Table 2.1 shows, nearly 60 percent of these FBOs are Christian, while, as already noted in chapter 1, "Muslim, Hindu and Buddhist NGOs are grossly underrepresented compared to the number of adherents to Islam, Hinduism and Buddhism worldwide" (Petersen, 2010: 5).

Among Christian FBOs, a significant number are linked to the Catholic Church, including the Vatican and the Holy See. This underlines both the variable roles and organizational capacity of the Holy See and more generally the Catholic Church, which sets the Church apart from, for example, Islam.

TABLE 2.1   *Religious affiliation of FBOs at the UN*

Religious affiliation	Number of organizations	Percentage of all FBOs
Christian	187	58.4
Muslim	52	16.3
Jewish	22	6.9
Buddhist	14	4.4
Hindu	3	0.9
Spiritual	25	7.8
Multireligious	11	3.4
Other religions	6	1.9
Total	320	100

Source: Petersen (2010: 5).

Although Islam, like Christianity, also spread in part through missionary activity, the historical details of its development led to organizational structures characterized by territorial and ideological boundaries. That is, while Christian missions were typically supported, implicitly or explicitly, by the governments of the countries from where they came, Islamic identity and interorganizational structures typically developed alongside the various nationalisms that developed in response to Western colonialism (Lapidus, 2001: 46–48). As a consequence, Lapidus points out, that "while there are numerous [universal] associations that operate for religious purposes, most Islamic political groups are in fact localized in national state contexts . . . National states define the boundaries of Muslim identities" (Lapidus, 2000: 38). As a result, Islam lacks a centralized, international organizational structure comparable to that of the Catholic Church although as we shall see in chapter 6, the Organization of Islamic Cooperation seeks to builds such a role for itself, albeit with only partial success. Furthermore, in addition to lacking an internationally centralized authority recognized as a legitimate representative of universalistic Islam (that is, no Muslim pope), the Muslim faith also lacks a more or less common model of religion-state relations. These characteristics of transnational Islam present significant barriers to collective action within international relations, thus leaving Islam at a "disadvantage in competing for resources and institutional access on the formal political terrain of the world polity as well" (Bush, 2005: 52–53).

Most FBOs active at the UN pursue justice and human rights issues and actively join associated campaigns (Haynes, 2013c). This is not to imply that such campaigns are only of contemporary or current importance. Florini (1999: 9) discusses the importance of transnational civil society for ending slavery in the early nineteenth century and in doing so emphasizes that the involvement of faith-based actors in relation to justice and human rights is not a recent phenomenon. More recent, more active and more transnationally focused activities of FBOs animated by justice and human rights concerns arose following the post–Cold War communications revolution centrally characterizing globalization today. In addition, in recent years, massively increased global migration helped to spawn more and more active religious transnational communities, some of which have justice and human rights–linked goals and aspirations (Levitt, 2004).

Once FBOs have "spilled over" the "borders of the sovereign state" what happens next? What do they do to go about achieving their objectives? We have already see that many transnational FBOs seek to influence justice and human rights outcomes via activities at the UN, EU, and elsewhere. They do this as they see such entities as a potentially crucial focal point of battles over international public policy, which impact upon values, norms, and behavior, crucial issues upon which faith actors generally have pronounced views. This section looks into this issue and refers back to this book's starting point, a general question: How do non-state religious actors affect outcomes in international relations? We noted in chapter 1 two main ways by which they might seek to do this. First, they might seek to pursue objectives via transnational networks, like many secular NGOs. Generally, increased transnational activities have received much attention over the last quarter century (Haynes, 2001; 2012), a period during which the Cold War ended and, as Voll (2006: 12) notes, "the structure of world affairs and global interactions" changed dramatically, as a consequence of globalization. "Both in terms of actual operations and the ways that those operations are conceived and understood by analysts, the old systems of relationships are passing rapidly." According to Arquilla and Ronfeldt (1999: ix), we can see significant changes in this regard "across many political, economic, and military areas, [where] international 'soft power' is taking precedence over traditional, material 'hard power.'" Second, there is evidence that in some countries, for example, United States, Israel, Iran, and India, there were attempts in recent years by non-state religious actors to influence foreign policy focus and direction (Haynes, 2008). The result, according to Fox and Sandler (2004: 168), is that "religion's greatest influence on the international system is through its significant influence on domestic politics. It is a motivating force that guides many policy makers." Overall, in both cases, the main tool that religious actors seek to utilize is their soft power, especially by encouraging others to accept and apply religious principles, values, and ideals.

The United Nations: a secular organization in a postsecular world

> As of February 2012, the total number of UN staff was over 37,000, and the number of UN agencies, bodies, offices, and departments easily amounted to sixty, each with its own staff and many with headquarters and field offices. In short, the United Nations is a huge entity with multiple facets and a plethora of forms, acting on every conceivable aspect of human development. Many FBOs often either refer to this organism as though it were one homogenous entity or complain about the confusion engendered by so many bodies all being part of "the UN." This is a very real concern because unless there is a deep knowledge of the system, which many in the UN themselves struggle to acquire, it can take a lifetime to understand whom exactly to reach out to, let alone partner with, and how best to do so. (Karam, 2012: 11)[4]

This quotation points, first, to the complexity of what I refer to in this book as "the United Nations." Karam emphasizes just what a massive *system* the UN is, involving tens of thousands of personnel and dozens of agencies and other entities. Thus suggests that any focus on the UN has to be selective as a comprehensive coverage of the entire organization is not possible in a short book such as this.

The UN was founded in October 1945, following the end of World War II. This was a time of emphatically secular international relations. This was not a novel position but reflected a situation extant for hundreds of years. It developed over time following the Peace of Westphalia in 1648, which marked the end of Europe's long-running and deeply destabilizing religious wars. The peace laid foundations of an irreligious international system dominated by secular states, with three secular cornerstones: the balance of power, international law, and international diplomacy. The nature of the international system was ideologically informed by the decidedly secular values of the American (1776) and French Revolutions (1789), and subsequent turn to nationalism, colonialism, and imperialism in the nineteenth and early twentieth centuries and, after World War I, a turn to economic nationalism and extremist ideologies of both left and right. Following the slide into global conflagration in 1939, the UN was primarily animated by a collective desire to rebuild collective security, so that such a conflict would never happen again.

From the nineteenth century onward, many issues were identified as global, not exclusively national in character and, as a result, states sought to develop collective, consensual outlooks and strategies. Examples include the successful fight against slavery in the nineteenth century and from the second half of the twentieth century, a focus on justice and human rights, including gender equality and religious freedom, as well as the fight against nuclear weapons proliferation and environmental degradation and destruction. Following World War II, the UN took a global lead in relation to such issues, establishing itself in the process as a key forum for the development of global public policy.

Reinicke (2000: 44) explains that "global public policy networks" are best understood as loose or even *ad hoc*

> alliances of government agencies, international organizations, corporations, and elements of civil society such as nongovernmental organizations, professional associations, or religious groups that join together to achieve what none can accomplish on its own.

Thus global public policy networks can bring together both state and non-state actors in pursuit of shared objectives. The UN is a major meeting point of such networks, concerned with a variety of objectives, some of which involve FBOs.[5] Despite this, FBOs and other religious actors are rarely accorded much attention in discussions of global public policy. For example, Stone's (2008) wide-ranging and widely cited article on global public policy includes not one reference to religion or faith. Between publication in 2008 and March 2013, Stone's article had garnered 116 citations on Google Scholar. Yet her ignoring of FBOs and religion more generally is not an isolated aberration. This is underlined by the fact that the flagship journal on global governance, *Global Governance*, featured *no* articles concerned with religion or faith between 2004 and 2013.

According to the Preamble to the Charter of the United Nations, the UN seeks to pursue improved peace and security, human rights, equality, justice, international law, social progress, "better standards of life," and "economic and social advancement of all peoples."[6] To help achieve these goals, UN agencies formally work with both states and non-states, including selected NGOs (Stone, 2008: 3, 15, 18). In its early years, the UN interacted almost exclusively with secular NGOs, before expanding operations to include institutionalized dealings with selected FBOs, via ECOSOC. This reflects the fact that numbers of international and transnational FBOs have recently grown, sharing a goal to influence global public policy. This development also reflects a situation whereby the UN is now "officially" willing and able to interact regularly with selected FBOs, whose position has been collectively enhanced a widespread religious resurgence, which informs morally and ethically informed values in debates about global public policy.

While the extent and institutionalization of current interactions with FBOs at the UN is novel, they are not *de novo*. The UN has long had an institutionalized relationship with selected NGOs—that is, those that conform to and support UN values. Article 71 of the UN Charter states that the UN will "consult" with NGOs in order to carry out related work through ECOSOC. ECOSOC seeks to facilitate "international cooperation on standards-making and problem-solving in economic and social issues" (http://www.un.org/en/ecosoc/). In addition, the UN Charter does include a reference to religion, albeit in the context of a fundamental UN focus: human rights. In this context, the UN recognizes religious belief as an integral aspect of wider human rights and freedom. A "Committee of Religious NGOs" was established in 1972, three decades after the founding of the UN,[7] followed in 2004 by creation of a "NGO Committee on Spirituality, Values, and Global Concerns."[8] The existence of these two entities emphasizes that even though the UN was founded on secular values, religious and spiritual entities have sought to influence it for over 40 years. Yet, it is only recently—that is, since the 1990s—that FBO numbers have grown significantly, focused in enhanced activity at the UN, including institutionalized FBO presence to UN committees in both New York and Geneva, as well as FBO interactions with many UN committees and UN commissions, including, for example, the UN Commission for Social Development (Carrette and Miall, 2012).

Overall, growing FBO presence at the UN reflects two main developments. First, there is a well-documented, recent increase in the significance of faith-based concerns in international relations (Haynes, 2013a). Second, there is increased general focus on "values," "norms," and "behavior" following the end of the Cold War and contemporaneous deepening and expansion of globalization. Reflecting this, many FBOs at the UN now have overt concern with various aspects of justice and human rights, including how poverty-stricken people in poor and undeveloped countries can improve their positions. However, achieving improved and more equitable international development is not simply a moral or theological concern. As Lynch (2012) notes, when FBOs ponder international development they typically move from initially moral dimensions to consider a highly material factor: "neoliberal competition of the 'market' [in] international development." From there it is but a short jump to begin to ponder on how more generally the conditions of globalization appear to encourage or exacerbate an unjust and polarized world, where the rich benefit disproportionately. In sum, the past 20 years—that is, the post–Cold War era—was a time of deepening globalization, which has coincided with what is perceived as a widespread "religious resurgence," characterized by growing prominence of ethical and moral (often overlapping with faith-based) concerns in debates about values, norms, and behaviors (Haynes, 2005; 2007; 2013a). Today, as a result, faith-based views and opinions are frequently heard in relation to ethical and moral controversies focusing on the nature and impact of post–Cold War globalization, in relation to increasingly polarized international development outcomes, as well as "climate change, global finance, disarmament, inequality, pan-epidemics and human rights" (Carrette and Miall 2012: 3). In sum, the focus, values, and content of global public policy at the UN are increasingly influenced "by the moral resources that 'religions' offer and agencies of global governance need an awareness of what religious actors are doing and sensitivity to religious difference" (ibid.).

Post–Cold War deepening and widening of globalization paved the way for the new, highly unexpected, opening for faith-based and spiritual energies in international relations, a development with variable impacts. Today's religious resurgence is not one-sided or easily interpreted. It can perhaps best be understood as part of a double-edged post– Cold War impact of faith-based issues in international relations, including in relation to global public policy at the UN. On the one hand, inter- and intra-faith conflicts in many regions and countries are a significant, maybe increasing, source of domestic and international strife. On the other hand, it is widely accepted that if "benign" and "cooperative" faith-based principles and practices could be applied meaningfully in relation to conflicts then such "emancipatory religious and spiritual perspectives in world order thinking and practice" might improve matters (Falk, 2004: 137). Falk conceptualizes this as a shift to what he calls "humane global governance," which he understands as a moral and ethical regime that may well involve religious worldviews. For Falk, a focus on global public policy that involves only secular (state and non-state) actors explicitly excludes an important component from the study and practice of global public policy: faith-based and spiritual dimensions of human experience. In this context, the UN, as the world's only universal international organization, potentially offers the widest available environment. The World Conference on Religion and Peace (sometimes referred to as the "UN of Religions"), asserted in 2001 that

> religious communities are, without question, the largest and best-organized civil institutions in the world today, claiming the allegiance of billions of believers and bridging the divides of race, class and nationality. They are uniquely equipped to meet the challenges of our time: resolving conflicts, caring for the sick and needy, promoting peaceful co-existence among all peoples (World Conference on Religion and Peace, quoted in Berger, 2003: 2)

Discussions of international religious resurgence and subsequent impact on global public policy overlap with another current debate in international relations: the extent to which today's international environment is no longer overwhelmingly secular but is instead increasingly affected by religious norms, beliefs, and values, leading to postsecular international relations. Reflecting these concerns, the UN has moved over time from a position where religion or faith were absent from deliberations to one where they are consistently prominent. Reflecting this change, global public policy debates and discussions at the UN underwent a shift in emphasis from exclusively secular and material to include moral and ethical issues, which frequently overlap with faith-based concerns.

Conclusion

This introductory chapter has argued that recent widespread religious resurgence has led to international relations having a new focus on how to understand the influence of faith on global public policy at the UN. Numerous, albeit mainly north-based and Christian, FBOs now have a regular voice in global public policy debates at the UN. Several overall conclusions emerge from what we have discussed so far. First, the UN has a strongly liberal secular agenda, whose focus, exemplified by the Universal Declaration of Human Rights (1948), lies in a range of justice and human rights concerns. As a result, the UN's liberal-secular focus compels all actors at the UN, including FBOs that wish to influence debates and discussions, to adopt "appropriate" UN-sanctioned language in their engagements with UN bodies.

I argue that FBOs often compete with each other on ideological—not necessarily faith-based—grounds. This implies,
for example, that socially conservative FBOs may well work at
the UN not only with other theologically conservative FBOs
but also with socially conservative governments and secular
non-state actors. On the other hand, liberal FBOs are likely
to work not only with other liberal FBOs but also with liberal
NGOs and governments, in pursuit of shared goals. In sum,
FBOs wish to maximize their influence at the UN and to do this
will typically seek to link up with allies—including, other FBOs,
secular NGOs, and friendly governments—which share their
ideological, though not necessarily theological, norms, values,
and beliefs. Some FBOs active at the UN manage to achieve persistent influence, via regularized and/or institutionalized access
to opinion formers and decision makers located in friendly
governments and IGOs. Others find it much more tough and
endure a kind of half-life at the UN where they take part in
activities but are doomed to stay at the margins of influence. Put
another way, some FBOs are less favored than others, without
consistent capacity to enjoy such access and associated potential
of building influence with significant players at the UN.

The chapters that follow seek to provide supporting evidence
for these assertions and more generally build an analytical
framework enabling us to understand the expanded role of
FBOs at the UN in relation to various justice and human
rights concerns. Chapter 3 examines theoretical approaches to
transnational religious actors, while chapters 4–6 look at what
FBOs do at the UN in relation to three issue areas: sexual and
reproductive health rights, human development in the context
of the Millennium Development Goals, and defamation of
religions.

3

Faith-Based Organizations at the United Nations: Theory and Practice

Today, faith impacts upon international relations in four main ways: widespread religious "deprivatization" (Casanova, 1994), pervasive return of religion to international relations, deepening and widening globalization, and expanding networks of growing numbers of transnational faith-based organizations (FBOs), many with social, socioeconomic, and/or political concerns. Increase in involvement of faith-based entities in international relations encourages development of linked "transnational" identities. This occurs when people who perceive themselves as belonging to transnational religious communities become involved in cross-border networks (Haynes, 2001; 2012). This can lead to increased intra- and inter-religious dialogue on many justice and human rights issues with ethical and moral dimensions, including women's sexual and reproductive health rights, improving development outcomes for the poorest people in the South, and fighting religious defamation (Toft, Philpott, and Shah, 2011). At the same time, however, expanded involvement of faith in international relations can also serve to encourage interreligious competition or friction between liberal and conservative FBOs (Bob, 2013).

To develop the examination of FBOs in transnational civil society, this chapter examines the theory and practice of FBOs at the UN. The context is the post–Cold War international environment, a novel, postsecular milieu, characterized by increasing globalization and significant return of faith, in the context of widespread religious deprivatization from the 1980s (Casanova, 1994). This was the background for many current debates and discussions at the UN, a forum that offers thousands of secular NGOs and hundreds of FBOs a place to be heard and an opportunity to try to influence global policy. As noted earlier, recent years have seen swift growth in numbers of FBOs registered with ECOSOC at the UN, from 180 to over 300 by the end of the first decade of the twenty-first century, an increase of 78 percent.

The UN is an important environment for global policy formulation and dissemination. This is because the UN is "distinct and to some extent delinked from national processes of policy making," which serves to highlight that "national public institutions no longer serve as the sole organizing center for policy" (Stone, 2008). Cerny (2006: 97) contends that this development is so significant as to involve a "restructuring of the playing field itself" with both "historical and structural changes to the 'state' and 'sovereignty.'" On the other hand, the UN does not provide a clear example of "authoritative" rule making; rather, the UN is a focal point of dissent, competition and conflict. Although some key UN bodies—notably, the

Security Council—have long attempted to develop "authoritative rule making and implementation," they have not been able to do so consistently or clearly (Haynes, Hough, Malik, and Pettiford, 2011). The result is that the UN is a highly contested milieu, a focal point of multiple, competing attempts to develop and implement global policy in an environment of significant disagreement about what those policies "should" normatively be.

Key areas of dissent in relation to global policy at the UN centre on justice and human rights. They concern the appropriateness and content of linked ethical and moral norms, values, and behavior (Bohmelt, Koubi and Bernhauer, 2014; Bush, 2005; Carrette and Miall, 2012; Carrette and Trigeaud, 2013; Carrette, Miall, Beittinger-Lee, Bush and Trigeaud, 2013; Haynes, 2013c; Martens, 2006). These concerns provide the contexts for battle lines drawn up between actors at the UN, including growing numbers of FBOs, often with polarized conservative and liberal views. The UN is highly contested terrain, with FBOs significant components in disagreement about how to build global consensus on justice and human rights and improve outcomes in these regard, especially for those deemed most in need of improvement: underprivileged people, especially poor women and girls and religious minorities, in impoverished countries.

The chapter is structured as follows. First, we briefly examine recent scholarly approaches to understanding the growth of numbers of FBOs at the UN. Second, we survey the emergence and development of transnational networks in the context of development of transnational civil society. Third, we look at theoretical approaches to understanding FBOs, and then briefly examine the Holy See, the Organization of Islamic Cooperation, and the World Council of Churches at the UN.

Research findings on FBOs and NGOs at the UN

Two major research projects have recently focused on increasing numbers of FBOs at the UN, investigating why this is taking place and what the results are. The first was undertaken over three years, between November 2009 and November 2012, under the leadership of Jeremy Carrette and Hugh Miall at the University of Kent, UK.[1] Following their investigation, Carrette and Miall conclude that

(1) religion is not always visible at the UN, [but] its influence can at times be substantial
(2) religious identities are more salient and significant at state level and can be a factor in UN coalitions, and
(3) examining religious NGOs reveals the necessity of examining other (non-NGO) forms of religion operating in the UN system and understanding how, why, and with what consequences different religious traditions vary in terms of influence

(Carrette and Miall, with Beittinger-Lee,
Bush, and Trigaud, 2013: 46)

A second salient research project, undertaken at the Peace Research Institute Frankfurt ("Religious NGOs [RNGOs] in the United Nations: Mediators or Polarizers?") runs from 2014 to 2016. The researchers' initial hypothesis was that RNGOs' activism at the UN "is often motivated by religious conceptions of justice," which tend however to result in ambivalent outcomes: "RNGOs may act as mediators or as polarizers in debates on controversial issues." A second initial hypothesis was that "religious NGOs adapt to their normative and institutional environment over time and thus lose their particularistic, polarizing edge." (http://www.hsfk.de/Religious-NGOs-in-the-United-Nations-Mediators-or.802.0.html?&L=10). In the current chapter and the three that follow, I argue that this hypothesis is not sufficient to explain all instances of FBO behavior at the UN. This is because not only do we need to take into account relevant institutional factors, it is also necessary to factor in sometimes diverging political worldviews and associated conceptions of justice that serve to guide FBOs' mobilization and their behavior.

It is important to build on recent research findings in order to understand why growing numbers of FBOs have a significant institutionalized presence at the UN. Apart from the context noted above of there being "more" faith in international relations now compared to, for example, the Cold War decades, it is also helpful to see expansion of FBO significance in the context of increasing presence and influence at the UN for transnational non-state actors more generally. Compared to secular NGOs, however, an institutionally significant FBO presence at the UN is a recent occurrence, becoming embedded and expanding only since the 1990s. Secular NGOs, on the other hand, have developed their presence at the UN since its founding in 1945. Their significance can be measured by the fact that today many "have access to intergovernmental meetings, present written statements, make speeches, and lobby for specific texts to be adopted." (Willets, 2006: 305) Initially, however, growth in NGO numbers was slow: over the initial two-and-a-half decades, "fewer than 400 NGOs were registered with the UN, and at any particular meeting only a few of these were active, mainly behind the scenes" (ibid.). It was not until the 1970s, in the context of a series of major UN conferences— on trade and development, human rights, women, and the natural environment—that there was major growth in numbers of NGOs active at the UN. This not only led to more secular NGOs active at the UN, but also helped expand "the range of issues addressed, the types of activities undertaken, the amount of media coverage, and the extent of influence achieved" (ibid.). In addition, Martens argues, institutionally the UN began to realize the benefits of working with NGOs and consequently sought to strengthen relations with them, opening up "for more interaction with NGOs and creat[ing] diverse ways to bring them into its system" (Martens, 2006: 691–692). Today more than 3,000 NGOs are registered as having consultative status with ECOSOC, while many more have some role in UN policy making. On the other hand, while NGOs are strongly linked to international UN-organized conferences and agencies such as ECOSOC, like FBOs they have no formal status within the General Assembly, the Security Council, the World Bank, the International Monetary Fund or the World Trade Organization. Many NGOs want their participation rights to be extended to these forums, but there is significant opposition to this among the UN's member governments.

> A second problem is the imbalance within the NGO community at the UN between the numbers of individuals from North America and northern Europe and the lower numbers from other parts of the world, particularly from Africa.
>
> (Willetts, 2006: 305)

Finally, according to Willetts, the

> Cardoso report, released in 2004, favored new guidelines and practices that affect NGO access to and participation in UN processes, and provides the basis for ongoing discussions about reforming the UN system for NGO activities.
>
> (ibid.)

Like expansion in numbers and influence of NGOs at the UN from the 1970s, the 1990s saw significant growth in numbers of FBOs. Expansion in numbers of FBOs was consequential to increased awareness of global social, economic, and political issues, including: (1) changing international conditions linked to the end of the Cold War and the dissolution of the Soviet Union in the late 1980s and early 1990s, (2) deepening globalization, (3) emergence of postsecular international relations, and (4) demands for a "new world order," where pressing demands for improved human rights and justice could be addressed. Because such issues were also ethical and moral problems, many FBOs became involved in connected debates at the UN, in a context where faith issues were acquiring more legitimacy compared to the Cold War years. In addition, the UN began to demonstrate a more accommodating attitude to "acceptable" FBOs in the context of a more general "cultural turn" in international relations. However, not all was harmonious. As Kayaoğlu (2011: 13) notes, "religious actors rarely speak with one voice and often target each other." To examine why this is the case and to see what associated disputes are about, the following three chapters offer case studies of faith disharmony at the UN. Chapter 4 scrutinizes the contentious issue of women's sexual and reproductive health rights, chapter 5 surveys disputes about human development in the context of the Millennium Development Goals, and chapter 6 surveys the fraught issue of defamation of religion. In addition, as with NGOs, while FBOs now have a persistent presence at the UN, they have no formal status with the key organs of the UN. Also like the situation with NGOs, FBOs at the UN are mainly Christian, based in North America and northern Europe, with far fewer from other faiths and from other parts of the world, especially the developing countries.

Transnational FBO networks

FBOs regularly participate in transnational FBO networks. What, if anything, is unique or puzzling about them? Put another way, should we expect FBOs to behave differently compared to secular NGOs at the UN? Of course, there is nothing new to the claim that transnational networks will try to use whatever influence they can to achieve their ends. Research into secular transnational networks by, *inter alia*, Florini (2000), Keck and Sikkink (1998), Price (2003), and Tarrow (1998), has consistently noted the importance of ideas, norms, and values in encouraging people to act in one way rather than another, which Nye (2004) conceptualizes as "soft power." Soft power is a crucial component of transnational non-state actors' attempts to influence international relations (Haynes, 2012). This type of influence wielding is not restricted to secular cross-border entities. Transnational FBOs also attempt to use any soft power they may have to help them achieve their objectives. It is not hard to see why this should be the case: such actors typically lack hard (economic and/or military) power and so must rely on other means of wielding influence. In doing so, FBOs are behaving precisely as the general literature on secular transnational non-state actors suggests. Note, however, that most of the frequently cited research into (secular) NGO-led transnational networks appeared in the 1990s and early 2000s, that is, *before* it became clear that faith was "returning" to international relations.

Tarrow's (1998) book on "social movements and contentious politics," is almost silent on faith-based transnational networks, a position that reflected accurately the then overwhelming concern with secular non-state actors in social justice and human rights. Tarrow's book does however have a few brief—mainly blood-curdling—allusions to the normatively shocking behavior of "Islamic fundamentalists." He claims that these people were at the time part of "the most powerful global movement of the early 1990s," willing to "slit the throats of folk singers and beat up women who dare to go unveiled" (1998: 194). However, this is a rather limited and one-sided contemporary depiction of transnational influence of faith actors and says more about Tarrow's lack of interest in faith-based transnational actors than about what such diverse entities were actually involved in, in the 1990s. This was also the era of the third wave of democratization and in several regions—for example, Eastern Europe, Sub-Saharan Africa, and Latin America—and both local and transnational FBOs were heavily involved in demands for more and better democracy (Haynes, 1998).

Like Tarrow, Keck and Sikkink (1998) are also leading figures in the generic research area of "social movements and contentious politics" and, like him, they have very little to say about non-state, faith-based transnational actors. While they are clearly aware of the *potential* significance of faith-based transnational networks, they refer—again, only in passing—to only one category of faith entity: Christian "churches," which they see as *potentially* major actors in advocacy networks. A third key researcher in this context, Anne Florini, edited a book on "transnational civil society," which does not include focused material on faith-based transnational networks (Florini, 2000). Her book includes only brief references to faith essentially as add-ons to secular, human rights, and justice campaigns in the following contexts: arms control/disarmament, the then rebellious Mexican state of Chiapas, the International Campaign to Ban Landmines, and Transparency International. Finally, Price's (2003) lengthy, often-cited, review article in *World Politics* ("Transnational Civil Society and Advocacy in World Politics") does not even mention transnational faith-based actors, much less analyze them as a feature of transnational civil society, which Price identifies as a politically important international phenomenon. Overall, as Levitt (2004: 1) notes, "while much has been written about transnational economic and political practices, transnational religious life is not well understood" or, it might be added, does not even significantly feature in analysis from some of the best-known scholars in this field in the 1990s and early 2000s.

Like the growth in quantities of secular NGOs in the 1970s, FBO numbers expanded from the 1990s. We have already referred to the series of six important UN conferences in the 1990s that collectively focused on various justice and human rights concerns and stimulated growing numbers of FBOs to engage regularly with and at the UN. Overall, these UN conferences were of great global policy importance and, as a result, thousands of (secular) NGOs, and hundreds of FBOs focused on and became increasingly incorporated into the UN system, via ECOSOC association. Yet, although the publicity and sense of engagement channeled by these UN conferences were very important, they were not, on their own, sufficient to explain growing FBO focus on the UN at this time. We also need to take in account three other factors. First, as already mentioned, expanded FBO involvement at the UN was linked to post–Cold War globalization, which generally encouraged cross-border campaigns on various justice and human rights concerns (Haynes, 2005). Second, there was growing concern in the UN about including "civil society" representatives in the UN's deliberations. Many governments and UN agencies, including the World Bank and the International Monetary Fund, were anxious to dispel the notion that the UN was essentially a top-down, government- and elite-dominated entity that exhibited scant concern with or had time for bottom-up initiatives and concerns. Third, in the 1990s the UN introduced and developed a growing number of procedures and arrangements with the aim of "officially integrat[ing] NGOs and their activities into the operations of the UN," including in the case of FBOs formal registration with ECOSOC (Martens, 2006: 692). The result of these developments was that not only secular transnational actors and networks but also FBOs that agreed to "play by the rules of the UN game" found it possible to embed themselves in the structures of the UN, to become parts of debates and disputes and, as a result, start to play important roles in global policy formation and dissemination, often as components of ideologically congruent coalitions, featuring both state and non-state entities with shared goals.

Explaining transnational civil society

When FBOs are influential, it is because they are able to wield soft power through convincing putative allies that their ideas are attractive and appropriate to help solve a defined problem. FBOs are not *sui generis* in this regard; they are not a unique product of the post–Cold War world. Historically, influential transnational ideas, both faith-based and secular, have emerged in response to domestic and/or international problems that normatively require resolution. Over the last 150 years, various transnational ideas have had great impact on international relations. Examples include national self-determination from the second half of the nineteenth century; revolutionary Communism following Russia's Bolshevik revolution in 1917; Zionism in the first half of the twentieth century, leading to the creation of the state of Israel in 1948; anticolonialism and anti-imperialism, resulting in dozens of new states in the developing world after World War II; antiracism, foundational for the civil rights movement in the United States in the 1960s and the antiapartheid movement leading to black-majority rule in South Africa from 1994; Pan-Africanism and Pan-Arabism, ideas that coalesced in the notion of "Afro-Asian solidarity," formative for the nonaligned movement, whose first summit was held in 1961; and, most recently, uncompleted transnational environmentalism and human rights and justice campaigns (Florini, 2000).

What these transnational ideas have in common was capacity to stimulate large numbers of people across state boundaries to pursue common goals, based on their shared norms and values. That is, such transnational ideas appealed to large numbers of people around the world and, by virtue of associated collective efforts, they were able to influence outcomes, sometimes significantly. Crucially, success or failure did not only depend on ability to link up with state power. Instead, as Thomas (1999: 30) notes,

> transnational actors represent—or are seen to represent by individuals and groups in the international community—ideas whose time has come, ideas which increasingly shape the values and norms of the international system.

Note that this does not necessarily imply that such values or norms are either normatively conservative or liberal. They are applicable to a wide range of actors with various motives for action, only some of which we might normatively commend or agree with. What is clear however is that transnational actors and the ideas they represent, for good or ill, today help to set, mould, and influence international agendas and outcomes. They do this primarily by adding to the lexicon and vocabulary of debate, providing sources of soft power in international relations, often informing ideas, norms, and values of what is often referred to as transnational civil society (TCS) (Glasius, Kaldor, and Anheier, 2006).

Tens of thousands of extant secular and faith-based transnational actors form transnational civil society (Glasius, Kaldor, and Anheier, 2006).[2] From the early 1970s, their numbers grew from a few thousand to an estimated 25,000 "active" organizations in the early 2000s (Anheier and Themudo, 2002: 195). Today, as noted earlier, there are estimated to be around 40,000 active transnational actors. Most are secular in orientation, although some have faith-based concerns as a central component of their *raison d'être*. Transnational faith-based networks can be influential motivators of, as well as participants in TCS, especially in relation to promotion or pursuit of various normatively liberal objectives, including peace, intergroup understanding, cooperation and human development (Haynes, 2012).

The concept of transnational civil society (TCS) has three main components. First, like domestic civil society, TCS encompasses a variety of non-state actors, with demonstrable social and/or political goals. Entities overtly connected to, or controlled by, governments, as well as profit-seeking private entities, such as transnational corporations, are conceptually excluded from TCS. Second, such groups interact with similar entities across international state boundaries. Third, TCS takes a variety of forms; many are secular in orientation, for example, transnational nongovernmental organizations with constituent groups in many countries, such as Amnesty International or Human Rights Watch. Examples also include organizations with a presence in various countries, such as the National Democratic Institute or the National Endowment for Democracy (Gagnon, 2002: 215–216; Adamson 2002: 191–192). Some are explicitly faith-based, for example, Opus Dei, a Roman Catholic lay organization. Overall, transnational civil society forms an important aspect of the globalization thesis, challenging the notion, central to the state-based "Realist" approach to International Relations, that states are *always* the dominant actors.

Instead, distinct from the insular concerns of most governments and political parties, the "cosmopolitan" focus of TCS
concentrates on direct relationships between people in various
countries. The growth of transnational interactions, impor-
tantly as a result of deepening globalization in recent decades,
leads to increasing spread and interchange of ideas and information between connected transnational entities. Lipschutz
(1992: 390) defines TCS as "the self-conscious constructions of
networks of knowledge and action, by decentered, local actors,
that cross the reified boundaries of space as though they were
not there." Thus TCS comprises groups and organizations in
different countries that work together to create dedicated
cross-border communities that: (1) pursue common goals via
national, regional, international, or global campaigns, and (2)
encourage development of goal-focused transnational coalitions. Attina notes that

> transnationalism is not just a matter of individuals and masses
> who feel conscious of being primary international subjects as
> they are entitled to civil, political, economic, social and cul-
> tural rights by positive international law. In the world system
> these subjects form *the international social layer* which claims
> primacy over the diplomatic layer. Today the chances of *social
> transnationalism* reside in INGOs whose members cross states
> and assert "pan-human" interests such as the promotion of
> human rights, environmental ecology, [and] international
> development co-operation. (emphases added; Attina 1989:
> 350–351)

In this view, "international society" is an agglomeration of
different issue areas, including justice, human rights, democra-
tization/democracy, human development, and environmental
protection. What Attina calls *social transnationalism* refers to
the multiple linkages between individuals and groups in different societies that share a concern with such issues, creating

what he labels the *international social layer*. For Attina, the "international social layer" is a line of contacts between societies operating and underpinning the formal world of supposedly independent states. Two key questions can be asked about TCS:

▶ Why does TCS exist?
▶ How does TCS influence international outcomes?

According to Held (1999), TCS networks exist because their constituents aim for certain goals based on shared conceptions of the public good, known as "cosmopolitanism." Such networks are bound together not primarily by self-interest but by shared values, such as a belief in the desirability of normatively liberal objectives, such as democracy, human development, and international debt relief for the poorest developing countries. Many scholars work on the implicit or explicit understanding that TCS is *by definition* liberal in orientation. That is, that TCS seeks the goal of better, more ethical standards of international governance by providing potential for direct links between individuals and groups in different countries (Bob, 2012; 2013).

Transnational linkages focused in TCS develop into networks of diversity and plurality that, taking advantage of new communications technologies, facilitate growth of national, regional, and global transnational networks with specific social and political goals (Haynes, 2005). In relation to the second question ("How does TCS influence international outcomes?"), it is useful to note that according to the political science literature, the core function of modern domestic civil society is to try to check the power of the state (Haynes, 2001). Of course, there is no global government analogous to domestic governments within individual countries, although the UN may aspire to fulfill this role. Unlike domestic civil society, transnational civil society is not *territorially* fixed, but is thought to comprise a field of action whose parameters are not fixed but can change in order to suit requirements of new issues and changing circumstances. In sum, TCS seeks to influence international outcomes by using networks of like-minded individuals to focus on shared concerns and encourage decision makers—both domestically within states and internationally, for example, at the UN—to make normatively appropriate decisions and, more generally, to help disseminate "correct" global policy.

The significance of TCS for international relations is that many people and associated organizations not confined to a single country, both secular and faith-based, believe in similar ideas and seek to achieve shared objectives, working collectively across state boundaries, and frequently focusing their attention on influential regional organizations (such as the European Union) or global entities (such as the UN) (Larsen, 2014; Bob, 2012, 2013). This highlights what might be called a "multiple issues" agenda encouraging government decision makers—once concerned only with "domestic" issues, for example, energy, telecommunications, food, agriculture, and the natural environment—to take transnational non-state actors into account in relation to various issues, which have in recent decades become internationalized, including the natural environment, human rights, justice, and democratization/democracy. This not only presents organizational difficulties in coordinating the work of different branches of government but also "generates political problems as a proliferation of newly created policy coalitions seek to influence policy" (Webber and Smith, 2002: 63–64). In short, there are now multiple channels of contact linking states and societies, both within and between countries, which impact upon both policy making and execution. Transnational civil society is central to the development of these channels.

Theoretical approaches to understanding the activities of NGOs and FBOs

The networks that comprise TCS share a concern with seeking to influence global policy formation and dissemination at the UN. According to Bob, "transnational activism" includes three "common phenomena": (1) non-state actors based in one country forming transnational advocacy networks (TANs) with similar entities in other countries; (2) these networks then seeking to influence ideas and policy in other societies; and (3) the networks seeking to affect international organizations and their member states as they develop global policy (Bob, 2013: 72, quoting Keck and Sikkink, 1998: 2).

Thousands of secular NGOs and hundreds of FBOs are now incorporated into the UN system via registration with ECOSOC. Yet, current theoretical approaches struggle to explain this increased institutional involvement. This is because, according to Martens (2006: 692), scholars tend to focus only on the impact of NGOs to influence the UN and "neglect other spectra of interaction between the two types of organisations."

International relations scholars suggest various theoretical models to explain why NGOs and FBOs seek to work with the UN and other IGOs, such as the EU and the OIC. In relation to international relations, Martens (2006) distinguishes two strands of "NGO studies": *transnational* and *transsocietal* approaches. Transnational approaches are models of international relations that understand NGOs as seeking to achieve increased influence "through various shifts from realist perspectives to pluralist images on world affairs. They have inspired wider discussion and research on the impact of non-state actors in international relations." "*Transnationalists* (see contributors to Risse-Kappen, 1995) introduce an elaborated theoretical conceptualization of the conditions under which transnational actors," including NGOs—and by extension, FBOs, impact on international relations. In this view, NGOs and IGOs are the highest form of institutionalized relations in their respective categories: non-state actors and groupings of states. Along with multinational corporations, transnational NGOs are said to represent the most highly institutional-ized forms of transnational relations since they often possess developed administrative structures, specific rules, and func-tions for associated employees.[3] Similarly, IGOs (together with international regimes) are the most institutionalized form of interstate relations.

Transsocietal approaches, on the other hand, are models of societal activism initially developed within national contexts and then applied to international contexts when it becomes apparent that associated transnational networks are target-ing regional and international governmental organizations, such as the UN, the EU, and the OIC. In short, transsocietal approaches are employed when trying to explain the emer-gence and significance of organizations that become active in regional and/or international contexts, rather than only national environments.

Martens (2006) contends that INGO interactions with IGOs such as the UN may be fruitful because IGOs serve as mediators for NGO activity. Two settings significantly influence transna-tional actors' activity and ability to act in this context: *domestic structures,* including the normative and organizational designs by which the state and society are formed and interlinked, and *international institutionalization,* that is, the degree by which international agreements, regimes, or organizations regulate a specific issue-area (Risse-Kappen, 1995; also see Böhmelt, Koubi and Bernauer 2014). The domestic structure model seeks to explain why non-state actors have varying influence in different countries; however, this does not account for the divergence of influence for different issue-areas within the same country. The reasons for this lie in the different degrees of international institutionalization in a particular issue-area: the more a specific issue-area is arranged by international cooperation, the more permeable state boundaries should become for transnational activity (Haynes, 2005). What has been neglected in such theoretical approaches, however, is that NGOs have indeed become an integral part of the UN system itself. In other words, mechanisms for *incorporating* NGOs and their activities into the frame of IGOs are not always acknowledged in such accounts. Böhmelt, Koubi, and Bernauer (2014: 31) examine a specific example of NGO activity at the UN: involvement in global climate negotiations as parts of national delegations. They note that "around 70 per cent of all national delegations include[e] at least one" civil society actor. Their explanation focuses on "international governance networks and legitimacy" in trying to explain NGO involvement in global policy. They also argue that governments "consider both constraints on government behaviour and gains in legitimacy when deciding on whether or not to formally involve [civil society organizations] in their delegations." This implies an example of "integrated" interaction. However, it could also be argued that government willingness to include NGOs or other civil society representatives in global climate change talks is linked to the fact that much technical expertise on this issue exists outside state control. Thus, to include such CSO representatives also makes sense from a resource perspective, as the state is able to benefit from research and technical expertise that it does not control.

While secular NGOs have been part of national delegations on continuing debates about climate change, scholars have recently noted that faith-based voices have recently become louder at the UN, and have become integral aspects of the UN system, albeit without a right to be involved in deliberations of the UN "big hitters," such as the General Assembly, the Security Council, the World Bank, the International Monetary Fund, and the World Trade Organization. Not only their recent emergence and development but also the inherent suspicion in the UN about the validity of their presence and opinions inhibits deeper and more comprehensive integration with state-focused fora. Beittinger-Lee identifies three modes of interaction—"immersed," "integrated," and "initiating"—practiced by FBOs at UN headquarters in New York (Carrette and Miall, with Beittinger-Lee, Bush and Trigeaud, 2013: 24–27). What characterizes each is "the degree of distance or closeness" that the FBO has "with the official UN procedures and processes." First, immersed involvement occurs when the UN definitively sets the parameters of FBO engagement and the latter has no effective ability to change the arrangement in their favor. As a result, when a FBO becomes involved in the UN via formal sessions and meetings, they are totally immersed in that environment and if they want to be part of the institutional arrangement, they must completely comply with extant rules and restrictions. Second, FBOs work in an integrated context when they function as "partners alongside other stakeholders such as UN agencies or member states" and as a result have a certain amount of ability to mould the agenda. Third, initiating involvement comes about when FBOs target what they do directly to the public, other non-state or state actors such as UN member states, the UN secretariat, or other institutional entities or employees of UN agencies (Beittinger-Lee, 2013: 24–27).

So, what we see is a swiftly growing FBO presence at the UN and in some contexts increased willingness on the part of the UN to engage with issues of relevance to FBOs. It is not clear overall how the UN regards FBOs. On the one hand, it is argued that the UN is neutral to faith-based voices, arguments, and campaigns. This argument claims that the UN provides an equal playing field for faith-based voices, but does not favor them nor does it necessarily endorse their (faith-based) arguments and objectives. For example, in his recent account of the clashes between the Christian right and liberal and left-leaning groups at the United Nations, which can be either faith-based or secular, Cliff Bob (2012, 2013) maintains that "transnational processes in themselves are neutral" toward different ideologies and religions. In a similar vein, the authors of *Religion and Public Policy at the UN* asserted over a decade ago that the United Nations provides an equal playing forum for inter- and intra-religious dialogue.

Another view disputes the claim of UN neutrality to faith-based voices. That is, while it is agreed that FBOs have undeniably increased their presence within the UN system, this does not mean a level playing field; instead, faith-based agendas at the UN do not necessarily find increased success, not least because many governments are wary of or hostile to FBOs and are unwilling to treat them as legitimate players at the UN. Banchoff (2008: 290) argues that FBOs' failure to achieve their objectives in relation to a mooted cloning ban at the UN "illustrate[s] both the importance of religious actors in world politics and the limits of their influence." Attributing this failure to state-centrism at the UN, Banchoff contends that the norm of national sovereignty, institutionalized within the United Nations itself, framed the terms of the debate and contributed to the outcome: a toothless and ambiguous declaration with no practical implications for the future worldwide trajectory of stem cell and cloning research.

(ibid.)

What this means is that faith-based claims based on faith-based arguments are fundamentally at odds with the long-term adhesion of the UN to the superiority of states and their associated sovereignty. However, as Kayaoğlu (2014: 62) notes, while this theory is not inherently implausible, it is clear that "the norm of national sovereignty has not prevented the United Nations from pushing for other types of prohibition regimes or human rights norms." As result, "national sovereignty alone does not suffice to explain the ineffectiveness of religious voices within the UN system."

The Holy See, the Organization of Islamic Cooperation, and the World Council of Churches at the UN

Geographically widespread deprivatization of faith affects outcomes, both within countries and outside them. FBOs are active in transnational civil society and, at the UN, involve themselves in various policy fields. However, at the UN, FBOs are not only focused on what might be called faith concerns. Instead, they may turn into *de facto* political actors with pragmatic policies that are more likely to succeed than when only faith-based arguments are employed to pursue faith-orientated goals. In other words, in order to increase chances of success, an FBO's faith principles may be pragmatically amended to include secular concerns and issues. As a result, the issue is *not*

FBOs versus the rest at the UN. Instead, it is to what extent and with what results do FBOs find it expedient to work with non-faith actors, which share FBOs' ideological proclivities, including both states and secular NGOs? This in turn relates to a key question, one we raised in the opening pages of this book: *Why, how and with what results do FBOs seek to influence global policy at the UN?* In the next three chapters I argue in three case studies that FBOs focus their activities at the UN consequential to an understanding that, as the largest and most influential international governmental organization, the UN is uniquely positioned to provide FBOs with institutionalized access to influential people, including leaders, diplomats, and policy makers (Böhmelt, Koubi, and Bernauer, 2014).

While a numerically large FBO presence at the UN is only two decades old, the UN has been active in global policy formation and dissemination since its founding seven decades ago. Some FBOs, including the Holy See, the OIC, and the WCC, have been actively involved with the UN for decades. Since its founding, however, UN structures and processes have been dominated by states, which are almost invariably secular actors seeking to make and implement decisions based on individual and collective *material* preferences and values rather than faith-based ones. In this secular and material context, how might FBOs expect to influence global policy? Evidence amassed by Leaustean (2013) about an important regional governmental organization, the European Union, indicates that, like the UN, the EU engages with the selected FBOs out of a determination to appear more open and approachable to a variety of actors from civil society, both faith-based and secular. It does not necessarily imply that the EU or UN are becoming more attuned to faith concerns *per se*, away from secular foci. Instead, the issue is about working with—and being seen to engage regularly with—civil society organizations, including FBOs, in the context of a "democratic deficit." For example, in the EU, certain Christian churches, such as the Anglican Church, present themselves as important civil society actors, advancing the argument that as they "represent" millions of Christians they have a "right to be heard" by EU leaders and decision-making bodies on many social and socioeconomic issues of regional concern (Haynes, 2014). Moreover, while the EU has no direct proficiency or capability in relation to faith, nor is it likely to want or get any, it *is* aware that secular and faith issues now frequently overlap. For example, various issues—including human rights, culture, education, and geopolitics—are now central to the involvement of Christian Churches and Islamic FBOs at the EU, concerns that have become more significant by being consistent in recent years consequential to enlargement of the EU and increased migration in the context of globalization and international crises.

At the UN, some FBOs—including the Holy See,[4] OIC, and WCC—claim to represent millions of people. The Holy See, claiming to represent 1.3 billion Catholics, has had permanent observer status at the UN since 1964, with the attendant right to attend all sessions of the General Assembly, the Security Council and ECOSOC. In other words, the Holy See is not a "typical" non-state FBO but is instead a state overtly directed by faith principles. The OIC brings together 57 mainly Muslim-majority countries, with a combined population of hundreds of millions of people, and claims to be Muslims' global voice. The OIC was founded in 1969 and its relations with the UN began soon after. Like the Holy See, the OIC has permanent observer status at the UN. Finally, the WCC, the umbrella organization for around 350 non-Catholic churches with tens of millions of members, was founded in 1948. The WCC established relations with the UN soon after, principally through the Commission of the Churches on International Affairs. The WCC has maintained a constant and active presence at the United Nations for over 50 years, with UN Headquarters Liaison Offices in New York and Geneva. In addition, consultative relations have further been established with virtually the whole family of UN-related agencies (including UNEP, UNDP, UNCTAD, World Bank, and WHO), although not with the state-dominated General Assembly or Security Council.

Most FBOs at the UN are not like the Holy See, the OIC, or WCC in terms of their size, influence, and membership. Many of the more than 300 FBOs registered with ECOSOC are relatively small and comparatively insignificant, without much individual diplomatic, financial, or ideological leverage. Some, such as World Vision, have impressive annual incomes, numbered in the billions of US dollars, while other such as United Families International filed an income of just $54,791 in 2010 (http://dynamodata.fdncenter.org/990_pdf_archive/570/5706 58097/570658097_201012_990EZ.pdf). Many FBOs, however, are faced with a fairly stark choice: engage in coalition building, and organize and work with partners, whether faith-based or secular, non-state or state, in order potentially to increase the likelihood of influence content of debates and discussions on issues of importance to them at the UN in the context of global policy.[5]

Put another way, FBOs that organize and work at the UN are *necessarily* strategic, goal-oriented actors, similar to other kinds of comparable organizational structures, including many of the thousands of secular NGOs registered at the UN. This is because, as Hopgood and Vinjamuri (2012: 38) explain, like secular NGOs, FBOs typically adopt two main strategies at the UN: *alliance formation* and *specialization*. They adopt these tactics as part of a strategy to try and achieve their objectives, as they must compete in an oligopolistic NGO "market." The point is that although FBOs are strongly motivated by faith, they still face the same challenges of earthly existence as confront secular NGOs: securing limited resources and maintaining donor loyalty. It is crucial for FBOs to achieve consultative status with the UN's ECOSOC. This is because this confers a key validity, a virtual currency necessary both to build alliances and "seek financial support from other organizations within the field." Faith-based organizations denied such legitimacy will find it very hard, if not impossible, to either obtain support from or enter into formal arrangements with other actors, including human rights NGOs, foundations, and states.

> This explains why even groups like 'Watchtower,' whose theological doctrines declare the United Nations to be an instrument of Satan, or the World Sikh Organization, many of whose members oppose affiliation with the UN for political reasons, have nonetheless held or aggressively sought consultative status with the UN.
>
> (Bush, 2005: 16)

In addition to serving as fora for debate over various social, socioeconomic, and political issues typically related to human rights and justice concerns, the UN and other international, and regional entities such as the EU, function as arenas where religious identities are legitimated, challenged, or otherwise negotiated. This contention can be illustrated by focusing on the array of FBOs that can be counted under the banner of the Roman Catholic Church. On the one hand, there are liberal Catholic FBOs, such as "Catholics for Choice" (CFC, founded in 1973 as "Catholics for a Free Choice"), which seeks both to defend women's reproductive rights and to downgrade the Holy See's position at the UN from permanent observer to NGO.[6]

Denounced by several Catholic bishops, CFC illustrates both a fundamental conflict and a question over what it means to be Catholic, who gets to speak for Catholics, and how to define Catholic perspectives on human rights and justice issues. Some Catholic actors, for example the socially conservative Catholic Family and Human Rights Institute, have very different—albeit "Catholic-inspired"—worldviews compared to Catholics for Choice. Muslim FBOs can also evince a conservative/liberal split. In this context, we can note the socially conservative Muslim World League, with close ties to the OIC, and the liberal and autonomous Cairo Institute of Human Rights Studies. These differing FBOs highlight a more general truth among FBOs: Within most if not all extant faiths, there are divisions between liberal and conservative viewpoints that are often captured in differing faith-based perspectives focused in competing FBOs' concerns. The veracity of this observation will be illustrated in the next three case-study chapters, which feature human rights and justice issues that highlight both inter- and intra-faith divisions.

▸ What does it mean to be a Christian (Catholic, Protestant, or Orthodox), Muslim, or Jew in relation to human rights and justice issues?
▸ Who gets to be the definitive voice of Catholic, Protestant or Orthodox Christians, Muslims, or Jews?
▸ Is there a definitive Christian, Muslim, or Jewish perspective on human rights and justice issues? If so, what is it?

As Bush (2005: 17–18) notes "Catholic identity is continually negotiated" through competing claims involving, *inter alia*, the Holy See and competing Catholic FBO claims, which are often focused within the UN. These negotiations over identity, beliefs, and goals are very important as they have the potential to influence relationships of power within as well as among religious groups. FBOs with formal ties with international institutions such as the UN via accreditation with ECOSOC can have significant input into these types of negotiations. Those that lack such access do not. Thus, FBO ties to and influence within international institutions, especially the UN, the world's biggest and most significant, are vital indicators of stratification among religious non-state actors in international relations (Barot, 2013).

This emphasizes a wider point of great importance to the analysis presented in this book, a topic we shall examine in the next three chapters when we examine case studies. The issue is that there may well be more ideological variation among FBOs that emanate from the same faith tradition than there is between faith-based and secular entities (Barnett and Stein, 2012: 23; Bob, 2012, 2013). As Berger notes, FBOs, even those from the same faith tradition, frequently compete with each other, at the UN and elsewhere, with individual FBOs pushing "for change from both liberal and conservative platforms" (Berger, 2003: 2). In other words, even when FBOs share a faith it does not mean that they necessarily see the world similarly, ideologically. The implications of this are profound, as differing ideological worldviews on, for example, justice and human rights issues, can mean that FBOs from the same faith tradition actually perceive each other as ideological foes.

Conclusion

In order to pursue faith-oriented goals successfully at the UN, it makes sense for FBOs to build alliances with a variety of actors, including other FBOs, secular NGOs, and governments. The main criterion for such liaisons is that of ideological compatibility: Do the partners share similar liberal or conservative worldviews in relation to justice and human rights issues at the UN? When examining FBOs at the UN, ideological polarization can highlight that faith is not a fixed category or value with consistent meaning and understanding attached to the term. For example, many conservative FBOs would probably agree that the nature of the UN system—which to them may appear both "too" liberal and "too" secular—is to encourage values commensurate with a "secular global order" that conflicts or competes directly with what they see as "appropriate" "Christian" or "Muslim" (or other religious) values (Bob, 2010; 2012). FBOs with liberal views, on the other hand, with their roots in various religious traditions, will likely regard it as very important to try to counteract conservative forces, both faith-based and secular, in order not only to advance what they see as for them *the* most appropriate faith view but also to put forward what is right in terms of an ideologically generated approach to understanding and influencing the world. In short, because there are often major ideological differences between liberal and conservative FBOs, even from the same faith tradition, it is not helpful analytically to work from the premise of a clear-cut, generalized, secular *versus* religious split at the UN between FBOs and secular actors (Berger 2003: 10). Chapters 4–6 examine this issue further in relation to three case studies.

4
Women's Sexual and Reproductive Health Rights

Conservative religious groups have for years engaged in clashes over family policy. Much of their activism aims to preserve traditional families against what they decry as an *onslaught of feminism, abortion and gender politics* (emphasis added; Bob, 2012: 14–15)

While health policy is usually framed as a part of the secular political domain, it touches upon combustible religious values and engages powerful alliances across religious divides. *Catholics and Mormons; Christians and Muslims; Russian Orthodox and American fundamentalists find common ground on traditional values and against SRHR issues at the UN* (emphasis added; NORAD, 2013: 1)

The current chapter and the two that follow share a common aim: to examine FBO engagement in various controversial issues at the UN. Chapter 4 engages with the topic of women's sexual and reproductive health rights (SRHR). The issue is especially controversial as both conservative and liberal FBOs lock horns on this key human rights issue: that is, "a woman's right to choose" *versus* the "rights of the unborn child." As the quotations above indicate, what Bob calls "conservative religious groups" focus on "family policy," incorporating a range of issues, including "feminism, abortion and gender politics." The second quotation, from a recent Norwegian Agency for Development Cooperation (NORAD) report, emphasizes that the SRHR "health policy" issue straddles the intellectual and conceptual division between secular and faith, bringing together both conservative and liberal entities at the UN in pursuit of certain goals.

Chapter 5 examines how FBOs engage at the UN on the issue of how to improve human development, especially in the developing world. Despite the global attention on the topic, surveyed in chapter 4, initially there was no explicit sexual and reproductive health objective in the original Millennium Development Goals (MDGs) of 2001. However, following the Millennium Project's three-year study on implementing the MDGs and a period of considerable activism, the integral link between reproductive health and development as originally set out at Cairo in 1994 was internationally reaffirmed at the World Summit of 2005. Finally, in 2008, universal access to reproductive health by 2015 became a late, yet important, global development target under Goal 5 on Maternal Health. Chapter 5 examines differing views between conservative and liberal FBOs on the "right" to development, with each highlighting the moral and ethical necessity of advancing the position of the poorest people. The chapter surveys FBO involvement in formulation and development of the Millennium Development Goals (2000–2015), a major example of seeking to improve outcomes in international development, a key global social justice issue, seeking to improve the lot of the world's poorest people. The case study in the chapter is on the stormy relationship between the World Bank and the World Council of Churches, which highlights their varying interpretations of what constitutes (human) development and how to improve outcomes in this regard. Chapter 6 is concerned with the polarizing issue of defamation of religion at the UN. It examines differing perspectives evinced by conservative and liberal FBOs and highlights ideological polarization between two viewpoints: "freedom of expression" *versus* the right of faiths not to be defamed.

Examination of these topics in chapters 4, 5, and 6 serves to highlight and illustrate often profound differences between conservative and liberal FBOs, both from within shared faith traditions and from secular points of view. It also surveys development of a socially conservative coalition of interest groups at the UN from the 1990s, involving both faith-based and secular entities, including both state and non-state actors. Overall, chapters 4–6 examine controversial topics at the UN, which have generated prolonged debate and discussion involving both FBOs and secular allies. The aim is not only to see how individual controversies fit into a pattern of conservative *versus* liberal conflict at the UN, but also to highlight, examine, and explain, on the one hand, ideological differences between FBOs and, on the other, to understand their tactics in order to try to achieve their objectives.

Women's sexual and reproductive health rights in international focus

When the Cold War came to an end in the late 1980s, followed by the unexpected dissolution of the Soviet Union and its associated Communist system a few years later, there was a brief period of optimism in international relations. A putative "new world order," following the demise of ideological polarization between the United States and the Soviet Union, emphasized an unexpected yet welcome potential for international cooperation to resolve pressing human rights and social justice issues. The international community, led by the government of the United States, sought a structured approach to resolving pressing global social concerns. Championed by the then US president, George H. W. Bush, the new world order initiative served as a springboard to a series of six high-profile UN conferences that took place between 1992 and 2000. Their topics were: "human rights" (Vienna, 1992); "the natural environment" (Rio de Janeiro, 1992); "population and development" (Cairo, 1994); "human development" (Copenhagen, 1995); "women and gender" (Beijing, 1995); and "social development" (Geneva, 2000). Each conference had a focus on human rights and social justice and collectively they were significant for a concern with how to improve the social and developmental position of females, especially in the developing world. However, despite the intention of bringing in a new world order, the conferences were chiefly notable for a fundamental lack of international agreement on what steps to take—and what resources to devote—to resolve pressing human rights and social justice problems. Overall, persuasive evidence emerged not of a wide-ranging consensus for improvement but instead its opposite: often intense disagreement, with views dividing along ideological lines, pitting conservatives against liberals, bringing together secular and faith-based entities and state and non-state actors.

The thematically linked UN conferences held in the 1990s highlighted that, as secular actors at the UN had long shown, FBOs can be *either* conservative or liberal on a range of human rights and social justice issues. It also became clear that in many cases FBO stances were linked to their ideological view of the world rather than being only a consequence of their faith perspective. This emphasizes, first, that FBOs from different faith traditions can manifest ideological preferences in various ways. Put another way, there is no identifiable monolithic faith position in relation to human rights and justice controversies at the UN, and empirical evidence for this claim is presented in this chapter and the two that follow. Second, the human rights and social justice activities of hundreds of FBOs at the UN can only be understood in the context of the growing activities of transnational advocacy networks, whose growth and development was facilitated by post–Cold War globalization. As a result, the UN became a key focal point—in some cases, a singular battleground—for competing faith-based networks propelled by transnational activism (Bob, 2013: 72). Over the last two decades, the UN has become the global focal point for thousands of cross-border non-state actors, both secular and faith-based, organized in often extensive transnational networks. FBOs use the UN as a focal point because they believe that by doing so they stand a good chance of wielding more influence than if they stand aside from it, and enabling them regularly to interact with like-minded ideological partners who share their views and objectives.

We noted in the introductory chapter that the UN has foundational "secular-liberal" norms and values, with little or no time for faith-based arguments or actors. To get round this ideological issue, FBOs find it sensible—indeed, necessary—to employ "UN-approved" arguments—that is, secular-liberal *not* overtly faith-derived ones—in pursuit of their objectives. Not to do so, is to invite failure. For example, regarding women's sexual and reproductive health rights, FBOs at the UN adopt one of two approaches, depending on their ideological perspective: conservatives refer to "family values" and/or "the rights of the unborn child" while liberals emphasize the importance of a "woman's right to choose." In recent years, as Sandal (2012: 67) remarks, while "religion has perhaps always been a force in politics, in the 1990s tensions between the religious and the secular in the political sphere became increasingly difficult to ignore."

The SRHR controversy at the UN is emblematic of divisions between normatively conservative and liberal views on human rights and social justice, disputes that are played out but never resolved. On the one hand, there is the "unborn's right to exist" while on the other hand there is a woman's right to do with her body as she sees fit. It is impossible to assert ethically that one view is "right" or "wrong," and how we see this issue is linked explicitly to our normative understanding of what is right and wrong. In recent decades, the issue of women's rights *versus* those of the unborn child have become a major international controversy and while the issue is not obviously one central to international relations concerns, the fact that related activism is now organized across state borders suggests otherwise. For example, the 1994 UN Cairo Conference was organized to discuss, on the one hand, the best and most appropriate methods of birth control—in the context of a swiftly growing global population putting an intense and growing strain on environmental resources—and, on the other, the question of how to arrive at more "female-friendly" definitions of human rights in a global context where in many countries females' rights were frequently overlooked, ignored, or undermined. Controversy attaching to these issues was highlighted by the decision of the Holy See, using its status as permanent observer at the UN, to "delay the discussion of reproductive 'rights' of women and to mobilize sympathetic states (including Saudi Arabia and Sudan) against voluntary choice in family planning" (Sandal, 2012: 72). Note that neither Saudi Arabia nor Sudan are countries with large Catholic populations—Saudi Arabia's Christian population is officially zero while that of Sudan is about 16 percent. The campaign led by the Holy See was not faith-based but emphasized a shared conservative worldview in relation to the women's human rights. At Cairo, the position of the Holy See led Egypt's then population minister, Maher Mahran, to state in exasperation: "We respect the Vatican. We respect the Pope. But if they are not going to negotiate, why did they come?" (Mahran quoted in Sandal, 2012: 72). Both Egypt and Saudi Arabia are majority Sunni Muslim countries and their division on this issue illustrates that their shared faith does not mean that the governments of both countries regard women's sexual and reproductive health rights in the same way. In sum, the alliance of the Holy See, Saudi Arabia, and Sudan on this issue illustrates that something other than a shared faith view facilitated their cooperation: a common perception not linked to faith regarding just what rights women should have when it comes to reproductive health and reproductive rights.

Both "reproductive health" and "reproductive rights" appeared conceptually in 1994 at the International Conference on Population and Development (ICPD) in Cairo. The conference was groundbreaking in that it linked population and development policy for the first time. The resulting rights-based approach to sexuality and reproduction facilitated a changing view: away from seeing people—especially women—as "agents" rather than "objects." This was a major shift from earlier international population conferences, where "family planning had been promoted as a utilitarian strategy to manage population growth" (Coates, 2014: 6). The Cairo conference produced a "Program of Action" (POA) that emphasized that both individuals and couples have basic rights enabling them to achieve a good quality of sexual and reproductive health, including safe and acceptable methods of family planning, prevention and treatment of sexually transmitted diseases, and safe maternal health care. The POA was particularly noteworthy as it acknowledged for the first time that abortion was a major public health issue and thus it was necessary to find ways of minimizing unsafe abortion practices and maximizing safe techniques and practices (UNFPA, 1994).

The Fourth World Conference on Women (FWCW) took place in Beijing in 1995, a year after the Cairo event. Beijing provided additional support for the development of women's sexual and reproductive health rights, in advancing the idea that they are fundamental women's rights. Specifically, the Beijing Declaration and Platform for Action declared that

> the human rights of women include their right to have control over and decide freely and responsibly on matters related to their sexuality including sexual and reproductive health, free of coercion, discrimination and violence.
>
> (United Nations, 1995: para. 96)

According to Berer (2004: 6), "sexual rights" is a "little discussed and poorly understood combination of the concepts of 'sexuality' and 'rights.'" A WHO Draft Working Definition, circulated in October 2002, defines sexual rights as follows: "Sexual rights embrace human rights that are already recognized in national laws, international human rights documents, and other international agreements. These include the right of all persons, free of coercion, discrimination, and violence, to:

▶ receive the highest attainable standard of health in relation to sexuality, including access to sexual and reproductive healthcare services
▶ seek and impart information in relation to sexuality
▶ receive sexuality education
▶ have respect for bodily integrity

▶ have a free choice of partner
▶ decide whether to be sexually active or not
▶ have consensual sexual relations
▶ have consensual marriage
▶ decide whether or not and when to have children
▶ pursue a satisfying, safe, and pleasurable sexual life."

According to WHO, "the responsible exercise of human rights requires that all persons respect the rights of others" (quoted in Berer, 2004: 6).

Turning to the term "reproductive rights," the following definition was agreed by the UN Program of Action adopted at the ICPD at Cairo, September 5–13, 1994, para. 7.3:

> "Reproductive rights" embrace certain human rights that are already recognized in national laws, international human rights documents and other consensus documents. These rights rest on the recognition of the basic rights for all couples and individuals to decide freely and responsibly the number, spacing and timing of their children and to have the information and means to do so, and the right to the highest attainable standard of sexual and reproductive health. They also include the right of all to make decisions concerning reproduction free of discrimination, coercion and violence, as expressed in human rights documents. (http://www.choiceforyouth.org/information/treaties/international-conference-on-population-and-development)

The definitions of both sexual rights and reproductive rights highlighted here indicate how both terms are intimately linked to human rights more generally, in relation to women, girls, and babies. Both emphasize—in almost identical wording—that these rights "embrace certain human rights that are already recognized in national laws, international human rights documents and other consensus documents."

In conclusion, SRHR encompass various rights, including information, services, education, freedom of expression, and freedom from discrimination and violence. Yet, despite the attention paid to the issue, especially over the last two decades, no international treaty exists that recognizes women's sexual and reproductive health rights as a core concept in international law. Instead, various links but separate foci have emerged—for example, public health and women's empowerment—which seek to create and disseminate international norms.

FBOs and women's sexual and reproductive health rights

> Conservative Christian actors constitute a particularly influential bloc wedded to a distinctly conservative social agenda, including in relation to SRHR. In this regard, liberals regard conservatives as motivated by pre-modern ideas about gender issues, family politics and women's health, working in effect to resist improvement or liberalisation of women's sexual and reproductive health rights. They represent a key factor in the resistance to SRHR, and work ceaselessly to contest, obstruct and delay the development of relevant UN agendas. Their influence does not reflect their number but is largely due to a striking ability to build alliances across religious boundaries as well as elicit the support of religious communities around the world. (NORAD, 2013: 1)

Two decades on from Cairo and Beijing, the global position on SRHR is unsettled. The two conferences highlighted emerging polarization between conservative and liberal views in relation to SRHR, which the quotation above emphasizes, and over time the UN has become the key global battleground. The issue become highly controversial, engaging consistent attention of often ideologically polarized FBOs. Between June 2006 and October 2011, Carrette and Trigeaud (2013: 16) identified 213

NGO/FBO-sponsored "side events" held under the auspices of
the UN Human Rights Council in Geneva. A majority of side
events involved issues connected to SRHR. Over half (53.52%)
were concerned with "women/girl/female" (71 events; 33.33%)
or "rights of the child" (43; 20.19%). (Other side-events topics
during this period included "peace" [43; 20.19%] and "religion"
[56; 2.29%]). The fact that more than half of the side-events
held under the auspices of the UN's Geneva-based Human
Rights Council over a five-year period were concerned with
SRHR highlights how the topic is both topical and contentious,
pitting conservatives against liberals, both faith-based and
secular. The topic brings competing groups of activists into
contention while encouraging the development of networks
devoted to pursuing their goals; and it is not of much—if any—
importance, it appears, just what the faith position of an actor is
or even if they share a similar faith-derived worldview. Instead,
it is much more important that they share a similar ideological
outlook in relation to family values/rights of the unborn child,
favored euphemisms at the UN covering SRHR issues.

According to a Norwegian Agency for Development
Cooperation report prepared for Norway's Ministry of Foreign
Affairs in 2013, "Muslim organisations and Christian NGOs
originating outside the Western hemisphere play a limited
role in the UN lobbying effort" in relation to SRHR, "except
in collaboration with three named conservative Christian
networks." Moreover, "Jewish groups are hardly involved,"
either in the network or on the SRHR issue more generally
(NORAD, 2013: 4). The three "named conservative Christian
networks," which NORAD refers to are all US-based, comprising (Protestant) "Evangelical," "Catholic," and "Mormon" entities, as well as a fourth "cross-faith" group (NORAD, 2013: 3).
The (Protestant) Evangelical network comprises five FBOs:

Alliance Defending Freedom, American Family Association, Concerned Women for America, Family Research Council, and Focus on the Family. The Catholic network is also made up of five FBOs: American Life League, Catholic Family And Human Rights Institute (known as C-FAM), The Holy See, Human Life International, and Population Research Institute. Three Mormon FBOs are mentioned as network members: Family Watch International, United Families International, and World Family Policy Center. Finally, the cross-faith network includes four entities: Doha International Institute for Family and Development, Howard Center for Family, Religion and Society/World Congress of Families, National Right to Life Committee, and International Youth Coalition. Note, first, that nine of these 17 FBOs have the word "family/families" in their title, while a further three include the word "life" in their name. Second, of the 17, two (World Family Policy Center and Population Research Institute) appear today to be defunct, and of the remaining 15, all but two (International Youth Coalition and C-FAM) have accreditation at the UN with ECOSOC.

The Doha International Institute for Family and Development (now renamed Doha International Family Institute [DIFI]) is based in Doha, capital city of Qatar, a country of just over two million people whose Muslim population comprises over three-quarters (77.5%) of the total. Islam is the established religion in Qatar (Kuru, 2009: 259), and Christians comprise less than 10 percent (estimated 8.5%)—around 20,000 people. Although DIFI is referred to as one of the four cross-faith entities by NORAD, in fact it is part of the Qatar Foundation for Education, Science and Community Development, a secular, not faith-based, entity. DIFI describes itself as a leading international institution that supports research, policy, and outreach programs that "promote the development of Arab families." DIFI has special consultative status with ECOSOC, which it achieved in 2009. However, lobbying at the UN is only a small part of the efforts of the activists behind a number of Doha initiatives to promote the "natural family." The institute is involved in "international, regional and local evidence-based studies relating to marriage and family structure, women, fertility and demography, child and family safety, and parenting," with the overall aim of supporting the implementation of the Doha Declaration. DIFI makes no mention of Islam or Muslims or faith but identifies itself as a family-focused entity undertaking (presumably) objective research on women, children, and parenting. The institute comprises three divisions: Family Research, Family Policy, and Social Outreach. In recent years, DIFI's work has included contributions to the UN secretary general's campaign to end violence against women; international and regional colloquia in partnership with most UN funds and programmers, including the UN Department of Economic and Social Affairs, the UN Population Fund, the Joint UN Program on HIV/AIDS, and the UN Children's Fund. DIFI has also provided funding, development, and writing of a range of publications, written by people from different countries and religious backgrounds on a generic theme: "The family in the new millennium," involving a pronounced anti-abortion stance and the championing of "pro-family" policies ("The Doha International Family Institute takes part in the First Arab States Regional South-South Development EXPO," 2014).

DIFI is financially supported by the Qatar Foundation (owned by the country's royal family) and works closely with influential US-based Christian conservatives. Such people have long been involved in the running of DIFI, making it a striking example of intercultural collaboration in pursuit of a shared agenda to emphasize, highlight, champion, and perpet-uate "traditional family values." DIFI was headed by Richard Wilkins, a prominent Mormon, from 2008 until his death in 2012. "The institute's modus operandi differs from more radical conservatives in its far less controversial language and more diplomatic mode of cooperation. Yet the centre is founded on the same conservative values" (NORAD, 2013: 7–8). It appears that DIFI seeks to become a leading cross-cultural agency pro-moting pro-family values and objectives.

In this respect DIFI finds it easy to link up and work with conservative Christian FBOs. For example, the Howard Center for Family, Religion and Society/World Congress of Families is a cross-faith organization with special consultative status with ECOSOC since 2003. The World Congress of Families is a network of pro-family organizations, scholars, and individuals from more than 60 countries. To date, six large congresses have been held, the most recent in Australia in 2013. WCF's initial aim was to build an international movement of "religiously grounded family morality systems" to "influence and eventu-ally shape social policy at the United Nations." Allan Carlson, a pro-family Lutheran, is the leader of the institute. He is a well-known defender of the "traditional" family in partnership with Paul Mero, a Mormon leader and head of an influential conservative think tank (Sutherland Institute). Together they wrote "The National Family Manifesto," which identifies itself as a guiding document for "a concise, coherent, compelling pro-family worldview and program of action." The manifesto talks of conservative faith-based principles but is written in secular language. It aims to be a key contribution to develop-ment of a conservative counter-discourse to "feminist liberal" perspectives on gender and family. The book is a mixture of religious doctrine and social science, and aims to supply an ideological component to Christian conservative "new family theology." (Buss and Herman, 2003).

DIFI also works with the National Right to Life Committee (NRLC), a cross-faith entity based in Washington, DC, founded in 1968. NRLC is the largest and oldest pro-life organization in the United States, with affiliates in all 50 states and more than 3,000 local chapters. NRLC's ultimate aim is to outlaw abortion in the United States. NRLC has been active internationally since the 1994 UN Cairo Conference, while the National Right to Life Educational Trust Fund was established at the UN in 1999. NRLC gained special consultative status with ECOSOC in 1999, initially as the National Right to Life Educational Trust Fund (NRLETF), NRLC's publishing arm. NRLC/NRLETF's main representative at the UN is the organization's vice president for International Affairs, Jeanne Head, a nurse. Following the Cairo conference, over the last 20 years, NRLC has been regularly involved in UN fora on women/gender, including: the Commission on the Status of Women, the Commission on Population and Development, the Commission on Social Development, the Human Rights Council (formerly the Commission on Human Rights), and the World Health Assembly.

Another significant cross-faith organization involved in pro-family issues is the recently formed, Catholic-based, International Youth Coalition (IYc). IYc was launched at the World Youth Conference in León, Mexico in 2010. Closely connected to a conservative Catholic FBO, C-FAM, IYc is regarded by C-FAM as the "real voice" of youth, a counterweight to UNFPA's liberal youth programs that allegedly produce "radical" youth delegates championing a SRHR-friendly approach. In response to the radical youth view, IYc produced a Statement of Youth to the UN and the World, as its own contribution to the International Year of Youth in 2010–2011, which was also a pro-family critique of the radical 1995 World Program of Action for Youth (http://www.c-fam.org/youth/statement/). An American, Timothy Herrmann, formerly of C-FAM, was appointed director of the IYc in September 2011.

From the above brief descriptions of leading conservative FBOs involved in SRHR issues, it is clear that conservative Christian FBOs are important components of pro-family campaigns at the UN. Apart from DIFI, whose engagement with the issue appears to be based more on cultural conservatism than faith, the organizations briefly surveyed emerged from conservative Catholic, Mormon, and Evangelical Protestant faith traditions. What of Jewish FBOs? Are they involved in these pro-family campaigns at the UN? Petersen (2010: 6) identifies 22 Jewish FBOs at the UN, 6.9 percent of the 320 entities she classifies as "religious NGOs." A few years earlier, Berger (2003: 9) identified 29 Jewish FBOs at the UN (9% of the total), including: Americans for Peace Now; *B'nai B'rith Hadassah*; and The Women's Zionist Organization of America, Inc. However, several of the most important Jewish FBOs are transnational umbrella groups, including the World Jewish Congress (WJC) and the International Council of Jewish Women (ICJW). Overall, however, "Judaism...has fewer adherents and a limited public policy impact" (Banchoff, 2008: 282) at the UN. It is also relevant that unlike many Christian FBOs active at the UN today, most extant Jewish FBOs have been round much longer: most were created in the first half of the twentieth century, that is, long before the days of major FBO involvement in global public policy issues at the UN, which developed from the 1990s (Petersen, 2010: 9).

On the other hand, being founded in the first half of the twentieth century and being relatively few in number, does not explain why Jewish FBOs are not involved in pro-family cross-faith campaigns at the UN. To explain why this is the case, it is necessary to establish what the position is on women's rights in Jewish theology. For example, the International Council of Jewish Women (ICJW), established in 1912, is an umbrella organization representing 52 Jewish women's organizations in 47 countries (Berger, 2003: 11). ICJW has consultative status with ECOSOC, and maintains permanent delegations in New York, Geneva, Vienna, and Paris. ICJW is also represented at the Council of Europe, the European Women's Lobby, the International Council of Women, the World Jewish Congress, and many other international and regional organizations (http://www.icjw.org/default.aspx).

The World Jewish Congress (WJC) is another umbrella group, which seeks to represent "Jews from the entire political spectrum and from all Jewish religious denominations…and tries to preserve the principle of unity in diversity." A third example of a Jewish umbrella group is the Union of American Hebrew Congregations, which is governed by a General Assembly composed of delegates who are members of and selected by member congregations in proportion to the size of the congregation (Berger, 2003: 12). Finally, Women of Reform Judaism claim to be "devoted to a broad spectrum of Jewish and humanitarian causes [and] furthers the teachings and practices of Judaism" (Berger, 2003: 14). Overall, these Jewish organizations "make few references to God or religion, focusing instead on the social justice teachings of the Torah as the basis for their advocacy-oriented missions" (Berger, 2003: 18).

These umbrella groups all come from the tradition of Reform Judaism, wherein women are believed to have more human rights in relation to control over their own bodies compared to conservative Christian worldviews. According to the US-based Religious Action Center of Reform Judaism,[1]

Jewish values affirm the right of a woman to self-determination, and while potential life is always considered to have value, it is never placed above a woman's health and well-being. The Reform Movement has long been staunch supporters of women's reproductive rights. (http://rac.org/advocacy/issues/issuereprts/)

Regarding reproductive rights, the view in Reform Judaism is that while all life is sacred, women are commanded by God to care primarily for their own health and well-being. That is, while the life of an unborn fetus is precious and to be protected, Reform Judaism "views the life and well-being of the mother as paramount, placing a higher value on existing life than on potential life. The view of prioritizing the woman's right over that of the fetus can mean that theologically abortions are not only condoned but even mandated." For example, a book of the Torah, *Mishnah Ohaloth* (7: 6), forbids a woman from sacrificing her own life for that of the fetus, and if her life is threatened, the text permits her no other option but abortion ("If a woman suffers hard labor in travail, the child (fetus) must be cut up in her womb and brought out piecemeal, for her life takes precedence over its life. If its greater part has already come forth, it must not be touched, for the [claim of one] life cannot supersede [that of another] life.") (cited in Leichtenstein, 2001). "In addition, if the mental health, sanity, or self-esteem of the woman (e.g., in the case of rape or incest) is at risk due to the pregnancy itself, Jewish teaching permits the woman to terminate the pregnancy. Because of the fundamental Jewish belief in the sanctity of life, abortion is viewed, under some circumstances, as both a moral and correct decision. This same belief underscores the vital need for medically accurate sexuality education and for high-quality family planning services" (http://www.reformjudaism.org/jewish-views-womens-rights-reproductive-choice).

This section has illustrated that even two decades after the Cairo and Beijing conferences there is no consensus among FBOs about SRHR. Conservative entities highlight the rights of the unborn child while their liberal counterparts emphasize a woman's right to choose. Since Cairo and Beijing, the UN has become the key global battleground for competing views in this regard.

Women's sexual and reproductive health rights: controversy at the UN

At the UN, both FBOs and secular entities rely primarily on value-based arguments to pursue their objectives. To make their case in relation to SRHR, conservative and liberal FBOs focus on family values and right to life *versus* a women's right to choose. The sense in this approach is to be found in the fact that the UN is traditionally a secular-liberal forum, and debates on human rights and social justice in global policy necessarily take place in a secular context. This results in the projection of associated non-faith based norms, values, and expressions, which, in the case of conservative FBOs, extends to their ability to express faith-based sentiments in the form of conservative non-liberal ideas, thus enabling them to bring into line their approach with the dominant secular-liberal discourse at the UN. In the case of conservative FBOs opposing what they regard as radically liberal SRHR policies at the UN, it is unrealistic for them to expect to make progress by expressing their arguments in faith-based terminology and values (based on community, personal responsibility, and traditional patriarchal understandings of the family and women's place within it). Instead, they couch their concerns more neutrally, emphasizing an ambiguous notion—family values—which enables them not only to overcome faith differences—for example, between different groups of Christians (Protestant Evangelicals, Catholics, Mormons, and Orthodox Christians) and conservative Sunni Muslims from various countries including Saudi Arabia, Egypt, and Pakistan (Bob, 2012: 37)—but also to find key "code words" (family, right to life) expressing conservative religious values in suitably secular language. Not to do so would result in only "limited access to discursive and institutional opportunities at the UN." (Samuel, 2007, cited in Kayaoğlu, 2011: 17). Consequently, for conservative anti-SRHR FBOs to be successful they find it essential to concentrate on countering the "pro-abortion"—that is, liberal—groups' agendas and declarations through blocking or weakening "pro-choice" language at the UN and in associated UN documents and publications. In addition, conservative anti-SRHR FBOs adjust the framework of their discussions by arguing for concepts like the "natural family" and referring to God as the "creator" in order to bypass theological differences and find non-Christian language (Kayaoğlu, 2011: 17).

Conservative FBOs' strategy in relation to SRHR at the UN developed from the early 1990s. The starting point was two UN conferences, with the themes of "population and development" (Cairo, 1994) and "women and gender" (Beijing, 1995). Preparations for and attendance at both Cairo and Beijing were foundational in creating, developing, and embedding networks of conservative FBOs at the UN. At Beijing, conservatives claimed that lesbians had launched a "direct attack on the values, cultures, traditions and religious beliefs of the vast majority of the world's peoples" (Bob, 2010: 2, quoting Human Rights Watch 2005, 84–85). Together, the two conferences marked the beginning of a concerted pro-conservative campaign in relation to SRHR, initiated and led by the Holy See, and involving Pope John Paul II, the Vatican, and conservative FBOs within the Catholic Church. In short, as Chao (1997: 48) notes, from this time "the Catholic Church became a leading actor on the conservative wing." The church's headship role propelled the then pope, John Paul II, a social conservative, to overall guidance of the international conservative faith-based struggle against pro-choice interpretations of women's sexual and reproductive health rights. The principal motivation for conservative Catholics was the presumption inherent in the pro-choice worldview that human beings have the right to decide life and death issues. In their own interpretation of Catholic teachings, the conservatives believe that only God has the right to make such decisions, that is, to choose whether a baby or infant lives or dies. Thus, conservative Catholic ire is directed against what the secular world would call progressive: "the notion, for example that humans share with God the right to decide who will and who will not be born" (ibid.). This is not to imply however that to be Catholic is *necessarily* to be conservative. Instead, there is polarization between conservative and liberal Catholics, with the former numerically larger among FBOs, including the Holy See, and their competition is played out at the UN. As NORAD (2013: 11) notes, "Catholic NGOs with ECOSOC accreditation range from the liberal 'pro-choice' activist group Catholics for choice (sic) to the most fervent 'pro-life' campaigners in American Life League."

Conservative Catholic campaign leadership is augmented by supportive involvement of other faith-orientated conservatives, including US-based Protestant evangelicals and conservative Muslims from various countries. Bob (2012: 36–37) refers to this alliance as the "Baptist-burqa" link and notes that "members of the 'Baptist-burqa' network...cooperate transnationally on policy goals."[2] The augmentation of the original conservative

Catholic-led campaign with additional conservative faith involvement highlights not only the constituent entities' shared conservative ideological orientation on this issue but also their diverse geographical locations that, as a result of globalization and the UN as a focus of concerns, are no barrier to organization and development of collective campaigns. For example, Italian traditionalist Catholics work with conservative Muslims from Saudi Arabia, Egypt, and Pakistan, while US-based evangelical Protestants and Mormons add their efforts to the "traditional families" drive. However, these diverse people are united not by shared faith but by a shared understanding that it is necessary to weaken or water down or, better still, block pro-women's choice language in UN debates, discussions, and any resulting documents.

Not content with sticking to the issue of women's rights, conservatives' pro-family concerns extend to denial of equal rights for Lesbian, Gay, Bisexual, and Transgender (LGBT) people, in the context of the conservatives' defense of traditional families. This emphasizes that it is not only one specific concern— women's sexual and reproductive health rights—which today animates and unites conservative Christians and traditionalist Muslims. This is because the more recent UN focus on LGBT rights—to add to the older concern with women's rights/family values—is also regarded by conservatives as comprising a liberal attack on traditional family values, which is itself indicative of a growing and wholly unacceptable "excess" of "liberalism" at the UN, thought by conservatives increasingly and unacceptably to inform global public policy. Bob (2010: 2) recounts the story of a Brazil-sponsored UN resolution in 2003 setting forth the proposition that homosexuals should have the same rights as heterosexuals. This propelled the conservative coalition into swift action, following the unexpected introduction of the resolution by Brazil at a UN Human Rights Commission meeting in Geneva. The Brazilian government's aim was to spread the notion of human rights as a universal right for all people, regardless of sexual orientation. Brazil's resolution expressed "deep concern" at violations based on sexual orientation, and declared that "enjoyment" of human rights should not be "hindered in any way" by a person's sexual orientation (United Nations, 2003).

Brazil's stand led to pro-family FBOs swiftly responding. For example, the US-based Mormon FBO, United Families International (UFI),[3] immediately dispatched its then communications director, Lynn Aldred, to Geneva to assist in the fight against the resolution's adoption. For UFI, Aldred's trip was essential because it was imperative that pro-family groups should "show up everywhere marriage and the family [are] under assault, [or]...those who oppose marriage and family will win by default." (Bob, 2010: 2) UFI was founded by Susan Roylance, a longtime pro-family activist, said to be the first Mormon lobbyist at the UN, beginning her work in the late 1970s. Roylance also attended preliminary meetings prior to the 1995 Beijing conference, which she referred to as "a wakeup call for those who believe the traditional family unit to be an important basic unit of society" (Tétreault and Denemark, 2004: 63). (Today, UFI's president is another Mormon conservative, Carol Soelberg). Other conservative Christian groups soon joined in with UFI, yet they collectively faced a serious problem. As FBOs, their influence was limited. So, the conservative activists turned to another wing of their loose-knit network: friendly states, including the governments of Egypt, Pakistan, and several other Muslim countries and the pro-family administration of George W. Bush.

Pressure from UFI and other pro-family entities in respect to Brazil's pro-LGBT resolution was not an isolated aberration.

Instead, as Kayaoğlu (2011: 8) notes, "With respect to state actors and religion...even secular states," such as the USA, "are not immune from religious pressures." Skillfully using the open nature of the US political system and the capacity to exploit both personal and corporate relationships, forceful pro-family FBOs learnt how to be effective in pressurizing the US government to adopt their preferred position on various causes at international fora (Haynes, 2008). For example, during the presidency of George W. Bush (2001–2009), several pro-family FBOs enjoyed strong administration support for their anti-abortion campaigns at the UN, being included in official US delegations to the UN on this issue. Among such FBOs, several of which were noted above as components of important extant conservative Christian networks, were the Mormon Church–affiliated World Family Policy Center, the cross-faith Howard Center for Family, Religion and Society, the conservative Catholic FBO, C-FAM, and the (Protestant) Evangelical Family Research Council (NORAD, 2013: 7, 23, 34, 35; Petersen, 2010: 13). Inclusion in the official US delegation took place despite the fact that several of the constituent FBOs did not have registered ECOSOC status, normally a sine qua non for FBO involvement at the UN (Samuel 2007, cited in Kayaoğlu, 2011: 8).

This is not to suggest that conservative pro-family FBOs have it all their own way at the UN. They are challenged by liberal, pro-choice FBOs. Globally, the women's pro-choice network brings together liberal FBOs; friendly secular NGOs; and supportive, mainly Western, governments, including from Norway, Switzerland, and Canada. The pro-choice network is coordinated by an umbrella group, WomenAction 2000, comprising 30 mainly regional networks from Sub-Saharan Africa, Europe, the Middle East, Asia Pacific, Latin America, and the

Caribbean and North America (http://www.womenaction. org/). WomenAction 2000's running costs are met by a group of agencies and governments, including WomenWatch, a UN "interagency gateway," the Shaler Adams Foundation based in San Francisco (whose strapline is: "women's rights are human rights"; www.shaleradams.org), the Canadian International Development Agency/Agence canadienne de developpement international (CIDA/ACDI), HIVOS ("an international development organization guided by humanist values" http:// www.hivos.org/about-hivos), and the Swiss Development Agency (http://www.womenaction.org/). FBOs included in the pro-choice network include: Ecumenical Women 2000+ and Catholics for Choice (Petersen, 2010: 13). Ecumenical Women 2000+ "is a coalition of denominations and ecumenical organizations at the United Nations who focus on the global intersection of religion and human rights with a gender perspective." The coalition works with both faith and secular entities—including FBOs, the United Nations, NGOs, and IGOs in order to raise the status of women and human rights (http://ecumenicalwomen. org/about/). Ecumenical Women 2000+ has 20 members, including The Anglican Communion, Church Women United, Lutheran World Federation, Presbyterian Church (USA), The Salvation Army, United Methodist Church, and World Council of Churches.[4] Similarly, Catholics for Choice, accredited to ECOSOC since 1998, also strives for gender equality and reproductive rights in partnership with various governments, including that of Norway, as well as the EU (http://www.catholicsforchoice.org/). Although a relatively minor exception to the norm, Catholics for Choice indicates that not all Catholic FBOs are dominated by the Holy See.

However, the most important player at the UN in relation to pro-women's choice is the (secular) UN Population Fund

(UNFPA). UNFPA has partnerships with more than 400 different FBOs in over 100 countries (http://www.unfpa.org/public/News/pid/1320). In recent years, UNFPA has sought to build links with various faith leaders, including Muslim imams in sub-Saharan Africa and Bangladesh ("Married adolescents ignored in global agenda, says UNFPA," 2004; conversation with Azza Karam, senior advisor on culture at the United Nations Population Fund, at Georgetown University, Washington, DC, November 20, 2011). UNFPA also collaborates more widely with faith leaders in sub-Saharan Africa, as well as takes part in educational programs and programs to advance women's rights in respect to SRHR.

Tyndale (2004: 6) notes that such collaborations between UNFPA and faith leaders became possible when both accepted that neither alone had the entire answer to development quandaries, including the lowly position of females in many developing countries. As part of its organizational program, UNFPA organized in Istanbul on October 20–21, 2008 a "Global Forum on Faith-based Organizations for Population and Development." The meeting drew together 160 key participants who had participated in earlier regional meetings—held in sub-Saharan Africa; Asia and the Pacific; "Arab states"; and Latin America and the Caribbean between December 2007 and September 2008. The Istanbul meeting brought together not only faith leaders but also representatives from various UN agencies, including UNFPA, World Health Organization, International Labor Organization, UN-Habitat, Joint United Nations Program on HIV/AIDS, United Nations Department of Economic and Social Affairs, United Nations Development Program, and United Nations Children's Fund.[5] The main purpose was to discuss successful practices and ways to move forward in partnerships with UNFPA in the following areas as they relate to women and girls: reproductive health and rights, gender equality, and population and development issues. The Istanbul conference ended with the launch of a Global Interfaith Network on Population and Development, with FBO leaders and representatives—from Buddhist, Christian, Hindu, Jewish, Muslim, and Sikh communities—pledging commitment to strengthen cooperation on human rights and development, especially as they relate to girls and women.[6]

Conclusion

Conservative and liberal networks, comprising in each case ideologically similar FBOs, friendly secular NGOs and supportive governments, developed from the early 1990s, focusing on differing approaches to women's sexual and reproductive health rights in the context of a global focus on family values and a woman's right to choose. Following foundational UN conferences in the mid-1990s, these competing networks developed into antagonistic, broad-based, highly competitive coalitions focusing on the UN as the key forum to fight about their conflicting objectives. A wider point that emerged from the chapter is that from the 1990s, several UN agencies began to take faith engagement seriously and sought to build relationships with faith leaders and FBOs in developing countries. We examine this issue in the next case study in relation to the connection between the World Bank and the World Council of Churches in the context of the Millennium Development Goals.

5

International Development and the Millennium Development Goals

It is a powerful idea—to tap the strengths of religions as development actors. Consider economics, finance and administration as disciplines that are deeply ethical at the core...they are about poverty reduction and employment creation. A vision without a task is boring. A task without a vision is awfully frustrating. A vision with a task can change the world. (James Wolfensohn, president of the World Bank, 1995–2005) ("James D. Wolfensohn Presidency 1995–2005: Faith and Development," 2013)

We have the opportunity in the coming decade to cut world poverty by half. Billions more people could enjoy the fruits of the global economy. Tens of millions of lives can be saved. The practical solutions exist. The political framework is established. And for the first time, the cost is utterly affordable. Whatever one's motivation for attacking the crisis of extreme poverty—human rights, religious values, security, fiscal prudence, ideology—the solutions are the same. All that is needed is action. (UN Millennium Project, 2005, p. 1; http://www.unmillenniumproject.org/documents/MainReportChapter1-lowres.pdf)

For decades, international development agencies and United Nations agencies[1] have focused on how to improve development[2] outcomes among poor countries, including the crucial issue of poverty alleviation. Yet, the fact remains that after years of effort and the expenditure of huge sums on the goal of improving international development outcomes, at least one in six of the world's seven billion people today lives in abject poverty. It is clear that whether on their own or working collectively, neither international development agencies governments nor the UN have all the answers to the question of how best to achieve poverty reduction and associated improvements in living standards for people living in poor countries. The two quotations above, from James Wolfensohn, president of the World Bank (1995–2005), and the UN Millennium Project (2005), both suggest that there is an untapped resource—faith, its leaders, and communities—which, if called upon consistently, could have a major impact on improving development outcomes in poor countries where most people are members of faith communities. According to Mahbub ul Haq (1934–1998), founder of the Human Development Report,

> The basic purpose of development is to enlarge people's choices. In principle, these choices can be infinite and can change over time. People often value achievements that do not show up at all, or not immediately, in income or growth figures: greater access to knowledge, better nutrition and health services, more secure livelihoods, security against crime and physical violence, satisfying leisure hours, political and cultural freedoms and sense of participation in community activities. The objective of development is to create an enabling environment for people to enjoy long, healthy and creative lives. (http://hdr.undp.org/en/humandev)

In their differing ways, both the quotations above reflect a growing desire to build development partnerships involving the private sector, NGOs, and faith leaders and communities.

The proximate context was both a realization that faith is an essentially untapped development resource and a growing realization over the course of the Millennium Development Goals (2000–2015) that their achievement would not be fully achieved by the time the process came to an end.

This chapter focuses on efforts involving two UN agencies, the World Bank and the United Nations Development Program (UNDP), and selected FBOs, including the WCC, to work together in the context of pursuit of the Millennium Development Goals (MDGs). The differing outcomes of initiatives involving the World Bank and UNDP highlight the potentially problematic nature of the relationship between secular and faith actors in this context, especially when they have different ideological perspectives making continued cooperation particularly problematic. Failure of the partnership between the World Bank and the WCC also highlights the great need for better and more coordinated relationships between secular development agencies and faith-based organizations active in this area; there is more likelihood of success while working together than while working apart. The overall conclusion is that there is untapped potential in working toward eradication of extreme poverty and hunger in the developing world, but it would be a grave mistake to expect that FBOs on their own can affect the needed changes. What is required for a greater likelihood of success is more robust and effective partnerships between secular development agencies and FBOs.

Human development and the Millennium Development Goals

The MDGs were announced in 2000. The first goal, presumably indicating its importance, was eradication of "extreme poverty and hunger." All eight MDG goals were to be achieved by 2015. When governments met in early November 2006 in order to assess the extent of progress made in achieving the goal of a 50 percent cut in food hunger by 2015, there was a serious lack of progress to report. Data released contemporaneously by the UN's Food and Agriculture Organization (FAO) indicated that there had not been a reduction as planned—but in fact an increase of more than 25 million chronically undernourished people during 1996–2006 (www.fao.org/). As a result, there were 850 million such people, more than 13 percent of the global population of 6.5 billion. According to Mulvany and Madeley (2006), this was "testament to how current global policies, far from working, are consigning the hungry to stay hungry." Failure to achieve progress on this issue, according to an NGO, World Forum for Food Sovereignty, was not due to a *lack of* but *too much* political will. The forum pointed to "advances of trade liberalization, industrial agriculture, genetic engineering and military dominance," claiming them to be the chief causes of the growing problem of hunger and poverty in the developing world ("Final Declaration of the World Forum on Food Sovereignty" 2001)

Pimbert et al. identify four main factors culpable for this situation: (1) the growing power of multinational corporations; (2) diminishing land and water resources; (3) climate change and deforestation; and (4) the impact of free market, neoliberal economic policies (Pimbert, Tran-Than, Deleage, Reinert, Trehet, and Bennett, 2005).

First, Pimbert et al. point out that in recent years small numbers of multinational corporations (MNCs) have acquired a large degree of control over the world's food system. These MNCs control not only seed, livestock, and agrochemical industries but also transport, processing, and retailing; and in the process they take a large and growing share of the price paid by consumers. The result is that farmers around the world— including the developing world—are compelled to accept falling farm gate prices. Some, as a result, face bankruptcy (Pimbert, Tran-Than, Deleage, Reinert, Trehet, and Bennett, 2005: 2).

Second, diminishing land and water resources around the world exacerbate both hunger and poverty. The situation is made worse by the apparently uncontrolled appetite for industrially produced livestock, typically fed on grains and starchy vegetables, a process that uses millions of hectares of land that could be used for food production for humans. In addition, huge areas of land in developing countries—employed for intensive farming in the post-1960s "green revolution" are now poisoned by pesticides; and some are also salinized by poor irrigation. The consequence is that yields are stagnating or falling, while pressure mounts to convert land to produce biofuels for the affluent (Pimbert, Tran-Than, Deleage, Reinert, Trehet, and Bennett, 2005: 15, 34).

Third, environmental catastrophes—including climate change and deforestation—are the main causes of both lower rainfall and drought in many parts of the developing world. These factors can fundamentally affect the ability of small farmers in the developing world to produce sufficient food for their own needs. This has become a major problem for food production. The problem is caused by less frequent yet inordinately heavy rainstorms, with declining numbers of trees, causing erosion, reducing soil quality, and producing meager harvests (Pimbert, Tran-Than, Deleage, Reinert, Trehet, and Bennett, 2005: 21).

Finally, according to Mulvany and Madeley (2006), "free market, neo-liberal economic policy has encouraged and justified the elimination of small-scale food producers in the developing world." The result, Pimbert et al. (2005: 1) claim, is that small-scale "farmers and indigenous peoples are seen as 'residues' of history—people whose disappearance is inevitable. Throughout the world, small farmers, pastoralists, fisherfolk and indigenous peoples are increasingly being displaced" by powerful economic interests.

In sum, those making efforts to decrease hunger in the developing world, including those linked to the MDGs, are fighting a losing battle against powerful economic interests, including MNCs. In addition, linked to post–Cold War globalization, the impact of the free market, neoliberal economic policies coupled with environmental factors including diminishing land and water resources and accelerating climate change and deforestation, is leading not to improvements in human development but to its opposite.

Faith and development

Today, there is increased interest in the role of faith in helping to improve development outcomes. Reflecting this interest, various UN agencies now seek to work with selected FBOs in order to try to improve development outcomes. To contextualize this development, it is necessary to recall that until recently faith was ignored or at best marginal in development theory and practice. Instead, secular worldviews were the foundation of conventional development understandings and policy, including both modernization and secularization theories. Over time, however, it has become clear that there is no compelling evidence to support the view that faith would wither away as a result of modernization and economic development and that a novel rationality would everywhere conquer "primitive" superstition and backward religious worldviews (Haynes, 2007).

It is also clear that faith is central to the lives of many, perhaps most, people in developing countries (Fox, 2008). While faith teaching and practice have diminished in significance in most if not all economically developed countries, especially in western Europe, faith continues to influence the worldview of those living in the poverty-stricken nations of the south. It is thus important to consider the ways in which religion can help as well as in poverty alleviation for poor people in the developing world.

To what extent can FBOs play a meaningful role in helping achieve the MDGs and subsequent initiatives? On the one hand, faith is now recognized as an important factor when thinking about how to improve development outcomes in the developing world. On the other hand, however, it is not realistic to expect that FBOs on their own could deal with serious development shortfalls, including dealing with endemic problems of serious poverty and hunger. To achieve this, what is required are basic policy changes—not so much in specific sectors or in the identification of new policy instruments—as in the way in which both development and its implementation are considered. In particular, most faith leaders would probably agree that the concept of *human* development should be placed at the top of the development agenda rather than being considered, as often appears to be the case now, as an add-on to the "most important" task of economic development *tout court*. Improved human development would however require in many developing countries—where state faculties are often weak or even, for some people, nonexistent—rethinking the very notion of policy implementation via both state and non-state development agencies. In extreme cases, that of state weakness or collapse, it is impossible to apply development policy in the conventional sense. Recent years have seen growing numbers of "failing" or "failed" states in the developing world, including Afghanistan, Iraq, Somalia, Liberia, and Democratic Republic of Congo. Such polities cannot realistically be revived by the techniques currently being used; instead they require new thinking about poverty alleviation and development more generally. External powers—for example, British troops in Sierra Leone, instrumental in rebuilding the state after that country's civil war ended in 2002—can play a vital role in facilitating state strengthening. Yet the task of political, social, and developmental reconstruction should primarily be through internal projects, involving local people and their representative organizations—including religious entities—rather than being planned and implemented by external personnel.

Of course, not all states, by any means, in the developing world are failed or even failing states. Yet, in numerous poor countries power is fragmented, finding its main expression in social networks, including those linked to faith. The consequence is that in some developing countries, development issues, including poverty and hunger alleviation strategies, can usefully be considered in relation to *social networks* rather than via formal—usually state—bureaucracies alone. It is important to stress however that policy makers should not regard societal networks, including those linked to faith, as development panaceas; they are *not* simple substitutes for effective bureaucracies and should in some cases be seen as partially *potentially* capable of carrying some developmental responsibilities. This is because faith-linked organizations are *not* professional state or development agency bureaucracies but *networks* motivated by different criteria, with different norms, beliefs, and values, derived from faith understandings. *If* it was a question of simply approaching faith leaders with a developed, nonnegotiable policy plan, complete with budget, then ineffective implementation would be a likely outcome. This might be because of the potentially corrupting influence of external injections of funds, perhaps serving to undermine a previously functioning network based on faith values. Instead, external secular development experts and their fund holders need to carefully build relationships over time with faith leaders and their networks, moving forward consensually to focus on how to improve development outcomes, especially poverty alleviation and eradication as a starting point for other development gains. In this way, ideas, plans, and programs could emerge consensually over time, with their foundations in the high degree of social trust linking members of faith communities.

Unfortunately, however, international development bureaucracies tend to have at least three major characteristics working against such an outcome.[3] First, development agency personnel, like other officeholders, may regard the size of the budgets they administer as linked to their overall prestige. As a result, such people may prefer to administer larger budgets—which may run into millions of dollars—compared to those that "only" run to hundreds of thousands or lesser amounts. In other words, an administrator with a smaller budget is likely to derive correspondingly less prestige from the task at hand. Yet, in many developing countries relatively small amounts of money are often preferable to bigger sums—not least because smaller sums may be easier to administer and actually achieve better results compared to large sums that can induce wastage or corruption. This is because in the developing world, societies have different textures to Western ones and, as a result, are not amenable to the same manner or using the same techniques (CGAP, 2004).

A second problem is that desk officers or unit directors based in Western capitals (or even in major population centers in developing countries) may not have much time or desire to spend lengthy periods of time getting to know key members of local religious networks, necessary to develop high levels of mutual trust from which comes the collective ability to develop crucial ideas (Gervais, 2004). Until recently, on their own admission, UN agencies such as the World Bank and the IMF had remarkably little contact with the worlds of faith and with the people who work in that world, whether globally, nationally, or locally. But if the World Bank and the IMF are serious about improving development outcomes in the developing world, staring with poverty alleviation, then it is necessary for them to change quite fundamentally their modus operandi. To achieve better development outcomes, including poverty alleviation, they need to develop *genuine* long-term partnerships with faith leaders and communities in poor countries. The starting point in what is necessarily a time-consuming and fragile process of trust building is that of representation, with secular and faith actors working together as equal partners, reflecting their mutually important roles in facilitating improved development outcomes. Throughout the developing world, faith entities own land, provide services such as health care and education, help poor people in need, care for orphans and disabled people, and support income-generating activities by farmers, fisherfolk, and slum dwellers (Olsson and Wohlgemuth, 2003: 157–158) Yet, many governments in developing countries are unwilling to work consistently with FBOs in pursuit of improved development outcomes—despite the fact that they often make significant yet frequently unsung contributions to welfare provision, including health and education. Explaining this state of affairs necessitates a focus on various political factors. For example, governments may prefer in some cases to privilege one faith over others or, alternatively, to adopt an emphatically secular agenda that rules out the very possibility of working with faith groups (World Faiths Development Dialogue, 2004). The issue is complicated further by the fact that while many FBOs claim to be politically neutral, this may not be true in practice—often because of sometimes complex relationships between FBOs and the state (Thomas, 2005).

The overall consequence is that FBOs' development work, including poverty alleviation, has long been "invisible" to external development agencies, including those linked to the UN. As a result, faith-based entities rarely feature in project analysis and documentation, general institutional vocabulary, research agendas, dialogue with countries, speeches, and internal staff training. Even today, with the partial exception of the World Bank, with its World Faiths Development Dialogue and Development Dialogue on Values and Ethics initiatives, it is unusual to find faith issues mentioned consistently or prominently in UN development agencies' literature or websites. While it would be incorrect to claim that the UN and other secular development agencies always ignore the developmental work of faith leaders and communities, it is more accurate to say that interactions between the UN and faith are typically sporadic and unstructured, involving specific individuals and as a result, they are rarely institutionalized. This situation is the result of either a lack of familiarity about what FBOs do, of preconceptions about the differing roles of the latter compared to UN development agencies, or a consequence of specific suspicions and assumptions that FBOs have fundamentally different goals compared to those of UN development agencies. In short, regular, meaningful, purposeful consultations with FBOs in the developing world have not been easy for UN development agencies to develop.

In conclusion, the brief comments in this section on relations between UN development agencies and FBOs are not meant to leave the impression that faith groups have the ultimate solutions to development shortfalls, including poverty and hunger eradication. But it is to suggest that "structures of belief, practice and institutional organization that exist in the name of religion are perhaps some of the least appreciated variables in the development process" (Pawlikowski, 2004: 17). Some in the international development community believe that there is a generic "faith sector" involved in international development, including in relation to the MDGs (Tadros, 2010). The implication is that there is a generic faith approach to development, which characterizes how faith actors approach the issue. But this assumption is actually unhelpful, as it poses a significant analytical problem (Haynes, 2007; 2013b). First among these is that it creates a misleading dichotomy between secular and faith actors by asserting profound conceptual differences between them, even though such assumed differences are often insignificant in terms of ideological and policy preferences. The result is that, seeking to identify and work on the premise of a "single 'faith sector'... elides significant differences among religious actors by grouping progressive, human rights–oriented organizations with organizations that might be opposed to the values expressed in the UN Charter" (Karam, 2012: 17). In other words, lumping together all FBOs interested in international development and assuming that they come at the issue in the same way and with the same beliefs overlooks sometimes profound ideological differences between them, which centre on what development is, what it is for, and who should benefit from it.

FBOs and the Millennium Development Goals

We saw in the previous chapter that FBO involvement at the UN often focuses on women's sexual and reproductive health rights. In this section, I focus on FBO involvement in international development issues at the UN, encouraged by the institutionalization of the MDGs in 2000 (Boehle, 2010). It is not however very surprising that many FBOs are interested in international development, as it is an issue intimately tied to many theological interpretations of the world. (For overviews of Buddhist, Christian, Hindu, and Islamic approaches to development, see Haynes, 2007: 18–24).

In this context, we can note the important involvement of various Christian FBOs—including, the WCC, United Methodist Church, Religions for Peace, and CARITAS—in formulation of the MDGs. In the context of "MDGs Post 2015," World Vision International, IMA World Health, WCC, Episcopal Relief & Development, Baptist World Alliance, Christian Connections for International Health, CARITAS, and Lutheran World Federation are active participants. Among Muslim FBOs, Islamic Relief (United States) has been active in both the MDGs and post-MDGs planning. Jewish FBOs are notable by their absence in relation to international development, in both the MDG and post-MDG contexts. Buddhist (Won Buddhist International), Bahá'í (Bahá'í International Community), and interfaith groups (Interfaith Center of New York, Tanenbaum Center for Interreligious Understanding, Temple of Understanding) have also been active. In short, announcement of the MDGs in the late 1990s led to a focus of FBO activities in seeking to help redress international development shortfalls, especially in the poorest developing countries. FBOs were interested in the general thrust of improvements to international development, and also had specific interest in the following MDG goals: arresting the spread of HIV/AIDS, and, in relation to gender issues in particular, achieving a significant reduction in infant deaths; providing universal primary education; and reducing adult illiteracy (Haynes, 2007; 2013b).[4]

Creation and development of the MDGs was in part stimulated by often egregious failure of economically liberal structural adjustment programs (SAPs) in the 1980s and 1990s. Despite the huge ideological and financial commitment from several UN agencies, including the World Bank and the IMF, SAPs' failure to overcome development shortfalls in developing countries where they were applied led to strong critiques from many quarters, including secular NGOs, grassroots movements and FBOs. A common accusation was that both the World Bank and the IMF promoted and supported a narrowly economistic conception of development via SAPs which, crucially lacking a holistic focus on human development, led *inter alia* to FBOs' disenchantment (Joshi and O'Dell, 2013). In the MDGs, both secular and faith-based SAP critics wanted to see a shift away from state and market-led approaches to broader, more holistic conceptions of development, focusing on increased interactions of civil society, human development, and grassroots participation. To pursue this different vision of development, many FBOs developed "human development" outlooks in the 1990s, which focused, *inter alia*, on opening development spaces to non-state actors, in order to augment development work undertaken by both international agencies and states. The result was that from this time, development-orientated FBOs became "legitimate actors in the field of development and humanitarian aid" (Petersen, 2010: 2). A World Bank study, *Voices of the Poor* (2000), was important in helping to cement faith's potential development importance, not least by the assertion that many poor people in the developing world had more confidence in FBOs than in their own governments. In sum, MDGs' advent in the late 1990s coincided with a new global public policy focus on civil society involvement in development—including activities of both secular NGOs and FBOs—which collectively sought to move on from the egregious failures of SAPs to arrive at improved methods to achieve qualitative international development improvements.

Like women's sexual and reproductive health rights examined in chapter 4, differing views on how to improve international development outcomes in the developing world led to competitive interactions between ideologically different FBOs. In chapter 4, we saw, on the one hand, the activities of a UN agency with an institutionally liberal outlook, UNFPA, which consistently provided strong encouragement for pro-SRHR entities and activities. We also saw the activities of a conservative actor, the Holy See and its allies, in trying to advance a different interpretation of SRHR. In the current chapter we look at international development in the context of the MDGs, and here too we find vying conservative and liberal interpretations. Joshi and O'Dell (2013) identify two UN agencies interested in international development with different ideological positions: the conservative World Bank and the liberal United Nations Development Program (UNDP).[5] Both the bank and UNDP have long focused on how to improve "international development" outcomes. Analyzing recent reports of both organizations, Joshi and O'Dell (2013: 260) conclude that the Bank's ideological outlook is characterized by a preference for "liberalization," the "private sector," and "privatization." The UNDP, on the other hand, has an ideological outlook identified via what they refer to as "leftist key words," including "basic needs," "full employment," "egalitarianism," "fair trade," and "redistribut[ion]."

We engage with two key questions in the remainder of this chapter. First, why was the outcome of the bank's engagement with the WCC ultimately disappointing? Was it the problem of the conservative ideology of the bank that made long-term working with the WCC impossible? Second, we examine the much more satisfactory relationship of UNDP with FBOs in the Arab region in relation to HIV/AIDS prevention, a key component of a wider improvement in development outcomes. What explains this result? Was the UNDP's liberal orientation not a significant barrier to the making and developing of partnerships with conservative Arab governments and FBOs?

The World Bank and FBOs

James Wolfensohn, president of the World Bank between 1995 and 2005, was a strong supporter of increasing the role of FBOs in order to improve development outcomes. There were two main reasons for this. First, Wolfensohn saw failure to involve FBOs in development as irrational, given their great importance to many people in the developing world. Second, the late 1990s was a period when the bank was actively seeking to engage with civil society, following criticism that it was not willing to listen to voices from below during the furor about SAPs (interview in Washington, DC with senior World Bank employee, January 23, 2012). It is not the case that Wolfensohn, an Australian secular Jew based for years in the United States, was primarily motivated by a faith-based worldview. His desire to involve FBOs in development was strongly instrumental. He believed that without consistent FBO involvement, there was a missed opportunity to harness potentially productive resources for improved development outcomes, in two main ways:

- ▸ *Bottom-up pressure on policy makers and consequential influence on policy formation.* This could occur by engendering and/or influencing policy makers' values and outlooks, in turn affecting the formulation of specific development policies.
- ▸ *Bringing together* or *dividing communities along faith lines.* This could either improve or worsen preexisting social and/or political conflicts centering on access to improved development opportunities.

The second bullet point suggests that Wolfensohn did not believe that building three-way relationships between governments, secular development agencies, and FBOs would always be unproblematic. Yet he saw the involvement of FBOs in development as rational for the following reasons:

- ▸ FBOs of various kinds—including, churches, mosques, faith-based charities, and movements—are important aspects of civil society in most developing countries. Their involvement in development policies and programs could potentially help achieve improved development.
- ▸ FBOs already play a key role in providing education and welfare in many developing countries, so it seems logical to involve them in development issues and outcomes.
- ▸ FBOs may share many values. Coming together in pursuit of development could help not only to achieve improved development outcomes but also, as a result, assist religious/cultural understanding in developing countries. (Wolfensohn, 2013)

During his presidency of the bank, Wolfensohn was the driving force behind the establishment of several initiatives involving FBOs. Wolfensohn personally created two faith-focused entities in the Bank in 1998: the World Faiths Development Dialogue (WFDD) and the Development Dialogue on Values and Ethics (DDVE). The WFDD was set up in 1998 as an initiative of Wolfensohn and Lord George Carey, then archbishop of Canterbury. WFDD's aim was to facilitate dialogue on poverty and development among people from different faiths, on the one hand, and between them and the international development institutions, on the other. "The focus was on the relationship between faith and development and how this is expressed, both in considering decisions about development policy and in action with impoverished communities all over the world" (http://www.wfdd.org.uk/).

The DDVE was founded in 2000, as a small unit at the World Bank whose purpose was to contribute to analytical work, capacity development, and dialogue on issues related to values and ethics. Over the next decade, DDVE served as the World Bank's focal point on the intersection of faith and development. During this time, the DDVE, initially headed by Katherine Marshall, followed by Quentin Wodon in 2008 following Marshall's retirement from the Bank, led a number of projects related to prominent development issues. These include economic crises in sub-Saharan Africa, with a focus on the difficult distributional trade-offs faced by various development actors in dealing with these issues. The DDVE was disbanded in July 2011 without replacement (http://web.worldbank.org/WBSITE/EXTERNAL/EXTABOUTUS/PARTNERS/EXTDEV DIALOGUE/0,,contentMDK:21966758~menuPK:5554943~pagePK:64192523~piPK:64192458~theSitePK:537298,00.html).

In July 2009, DDVE and WFDD jointly hosted a high-level meeting in Accra, Ghana, bringing together faith leaders, including Lord Carey and Archbishop Robert Aboagye-Mensah, the presiding bishop of the Methodist Church of

Ghana, who opened the meeting. Other faith leaders present included Rabi Saperstein and Cardinal Theodore McCarrick from the United States, Archbishop Martin from Ireland, and Imam Umair Ahmed Ilyasi, the secretary general of the All India Organization of Imams and Mosques. In sum, the Accra meeting brought together 85 faith leaders and development practitioners from 28 countries, along with senior World Bank staff and key development partners.

The Accra meeting built on four earlier meetings hosted at Lambeth Palace in London, England in 1998, 1999, and 2002, and in Dublin, Ireland in 2005. Earlier meetings convened a wide range of faith and interfaith leaders, and sparked momentum for better coordination between the faith-based and mainstream development communities, encouraged exchange of practices, and targeted advocacy for effective development policy and an increase in investments in development. The Accra meeting focused on issues related to the developmental role of FBOs and governments in the developing world, as well as other partners in service delivery (among others for education and health) with a focus on fragile states. Empirical evidence suggests that in some post-conflict countries, FBOs provide a large share of the education and health services used by the population. In many instances, governments rely on FBOs in other areas or sectors as well ("Economic crisis prompts expanded development role for faith-based groups— World Bank," 2009 [Press Release No: 2010/010/HDN])

The World Bank and the World Council of Churches

Following creation of WFDD and DDVE, and augmenting high-level meetings in England, Ireland, and Ghana, the Bank sought actively to discuss development problems and prospects in the poor countries with selected FBOs. In this context, following initial informal discussions, the Bank began a formal dialogue with the WCC—called "encounters"—in early 2002. Regular encounters continued until August 2008. Since then, however, no further meetings have taken place between the Bank and the WCC and, at the current time (mid-2014), none are planned or projected ("The WCC-IMF-WB high-level encounter," 2004). A six-year hiatus between meetings when initially they were regularly held, at least once a year, looks like a communication breakdown.

Before seeking to answer this question, it is useful to provide some background information on the WCC. The WCC describes itself as "a fellowship of churches which confess the Lord Jesus Christ as God and Saviour according to the scriptures, and therefore seek to fulfill together their common calling to the glory of the one God, Father, Son and Holy Spirit." The WCC

> is a community of churches on the way to visible unity in one faith and one eucharistic fellowship, expressed in worship and in common life in Christ. It seeks to advance towards this unity, as Jesus prayed for his followers, 'so that the world may believe.'
>
> (John 17:21) (http://www.oikoumene.org /en/about-us)

Organizationally, the WCC is an umbrella organization of 349 churches,[6] denominations and church fellowships from more than 110 countries and territories representing over half a billion Christians. Part of a broader Geneva-based ecumenical movement, the WCC is engaged in issues relating to poverty reduction, including in areas such as trade liberalization, governance, and post-conflict.

Between 2002 and 2008, the World Bank engaged in regular dialogue with the WCC. These encounters examined issues around institutional governance and accountability, participation of civil society in development processes, the respective roles of the public and private sector in poverty alleviation, and the challenges of globalization. Throughout this dialogue with WCC, the World Bank was encouraged to reexamine its concepts of development and evolving institutional mandates. The last encounter took place in Accra, Ghana in August 2008.

Why was there a cessation of dialogue between the Bank and the WCC following initially promising beginnings in the early 2000s? The first point is that the WCC was all along skeptical about the benefit of dialogue with the bank, expressing "far-ranging reservations about the motivations, governance structures, policies, and programs of the Bretton Woods institutions," including the bank (Marshall and Van Saanen, 2007: 196).

Second, there was no ideological affinity between the Bank and the WCC. Their incompatibility in this regard was highlighted in a hard-hitting WCC publication, *Lead Us Not into Temptation*, published in December 2001.

The 54-page booklet is basically a diatribe against the pernicious effects of economic globalization and the role of certain international agencies, including the World Bank and the IMF, in this process. The report is a direct result of the WCC being approached by the Bank and the IMF to enter into "dialogue on issues related to poverty and the economy in general." How then, the WCC asks rhetorically, should churches respond? Or to put it in the words of the 1998 WCC Assembly held at Harare Zimbabwe: "How do we live our faith in the context of globalisation?"

The aim of the report is twofold. First, it seeks

> to tease out and clarify some of the answers to this question. Its purpose is to equip the ecumenical family of churches with this background document that will enable them to respond appropriately to the challenge of globalisation and in particular to undertake a fresh critical review of economic and social questions that confront us today.

Second, for

> those grappling with the impact of globalisation and how international financial institutions (IFIs) affect the world's poor, Luke's brief account of the meeting between Jesus and Zacchaeus is a powerful story (Lk. 19.1–10). Upon reflection, what seems like a simple invitation becomes more complex. Why would Jesus make it a point to willingly and publicly enter into dialogue with someone whose sole purpose is to profit on the backs of others? What could the two possibly talk about? What if anything could be gained by such an encounter? Because the process of globalization is understood and interpreted in a variety of ways between the ecumenical and secular family it is clear that this document is essential if we are to continue in the ecumenical struggle for the attainment of a just and sustainable earth. There is also today a great deal of ambiguity in how the churches respond to the process of globalisation in general and to international financial institutions in particular.
>
> (World Council of Churches, 2001: 1–2)

In January 2003, the WCC presented churches' response to the policies of international financial institutions at the Third World Social Forum (WSF), Porto Alegre, Brazil. The WCC based its presentation on the arguments first presented in *Lead Us Not into Temptation*, published a year earlier. The main argument was that a leopard cannot change its spots: although both the Bank the IMF purported to be interested in engaging with FBOs in order to try to sort out development shortfall, in reality, the WCC averred, there was no sincere desire to change either how the Bank and the IMF worked or to accept that poverty alleviation and improvements in human development ultimately depended on fundamental changes to the structure and nature of the global economy. Unless, or until, such a change was deemed by the Bank and the IMF to be essential, no significant improvements were possible (http://www.oikoumene.org /en/resources/documents/wcc-programmes/public-witness-addressing-power-affirming-peace/poverty-wealth-and-ecology /neoliberal-paradigm/lead-us-not-into-temptation).

In response to the question "Why did the World Bank/WCC relationship fail to develop satisfactorily?" the answer is surely that each side had fundamentally different views of the nature of the global economy and the steps needed to bring about progressive changes to development outcomes. For the Bank, there needed to be a more efficient use of available resources without the need for fundamental changes to how the global economy was structured and run. For the WCC, it was essential for the world's poorest people to see their development positions improved significantly and consistently—and this could not happen, the WCC averred, without fundamental change. In short, while sharing similar visions of improvement to the global economy—not least being fundamentally improving the development position of the world's poorest people—the two sides could not agree ideologically on what was necessary to enable the desired changes to occur. On the one hand, the two organizations had apparently incompatible worldviews, which made it impossible for them to work together over time. Second, there was a strong "secularist" bias within the top echelons of the Bank. This meant that very few senior Bank figures openly sided with Wolfensohn in his pro-faith initiative. Third, many Bank employees—at both junior and senior levels— were uncertain about how exactly faith could be factored into development initiatives, including how the relationship with the WCC could lead practically to better development outcomes. Linked to this was a concern expressed by several senior Bank operatives. They stated the belief that improving development outcomes is most likely to be achieved through secular development initiatives and that faith issues are *inherently* divisive, frequently leading to complications and strife within developing countries (interviews with former and current senior World Bank employees, January 25, 26, 27, 2012).

An additional factor is that the conservative orientation of the Bank—focusing on issues such as liberalization, the private sector, and privatization—did not chime at all well with the WCC's pro-poor outlook, which corresponded to the shift in focus of the WCC from the north to the developing world, as the WCC became increasingly a south-led-and-run entity. The WCC groups together churches, denominations, and church fellowships from more than 100 countries, representing over 500 million individual Christians from non-Roman Catholic traditions. In 2014, the WCC comprised 349 member churches, with the majority coming from sub-Saharan Africa, Asia, Latin America and the Caribbean, the Middle East, and the Pacific. This contrasts from when the WCC was founded in 1948, when member churches mostly came from Europe and North America. The WCC's ideological position can be seen in the following WCC mission statement, whereby member churches:

- are called to the goal of visible unity in one faith and one eucharistic fellowship;
- promote their common witness in work for mission and evangelism;
- *engage in Christian service by serving human need, breaking down barriers between people, seeking justice and peace, and* upholding the integrity of creation; and

▸ foster renewal in unity, worship, mission and service. (emphasis added; "About us. What is the World Council of Churches," 2013; http://www.oikoumene.org/en/about-us)

Thus, whereas the language of the Bank emphasizes the perceived desirability of liberalization and privatization, that of the WCC stresses the importance of "serving human need" and "seeking justice and peace." These incompatible goals were clearly not conducive to developing a long-term, mutually beneficial relationship between the Bank and the WCC, despite an initially promising relationship emerging in the context of the MDGs.

The United Nations Development Program and FBOs in the Arab world

Failure of the Bank's relationship with the WCC does not imply that UN agencies are generally or generically unable to develop satisfactory relations with faith entities. In this respect, the MDGs were an important practical "shopping list" of goals. Whereas, as noted in chapter 4, UNFPA developed a close relationship with women's pro-choice faith entities, united in pursuit of the third MDG goal ("Promote gender equality and empower women"), the UNDP works closely with often conservative faith leaders in the Arab world, especially in developing shared initiatives pertaining to MDG goal number 6: "Combat HIV/AIDS, malaria and other diseases." On the face of it, this initiative might appear surprising, given the general reputation for "conservatism" that faith leaders in the Arab world have, especially in the West. Despite this, since 2004 a UNDP-led campaign has worked to try to end the stigma of HIV/AIDS in the Arab world. An initial meeting in December 2004, bringing together both Muslim and Christian leaders and FBO representatives, was followed two years by the "Second Regional Religious Leaders' Forum in Response to AIDS in the Arab States," held in Cairo between November 6–9, 2006. The meeting led to the Cairo Declaration, signed by 80 Muslim and Christian leaders, including the Sheikh of Al-Azhar, perhaps the most important (Sunni) Islamic institution, as well as the Coptic Pope, faith leader of some eight million Egyptian Coptic Christians, around 10 percent of Egypt's population. The agreement was a ground-breaking step that not only signified important practical efforts to deal the scourge of HIV/AIDS in Arab countries but also more generally served to increase interfaith cooperation in trying to respond more generally to regional development challenges. Over the next few years, the initiative developed into the CHAHAMA initiative, "a network of faith based organizations and leaders responding to AIDS in the Arab region" (UNDP /HIV/AIDS Regional Program in the Arab States, 2006).

In November 2010, Joseph Diess, president of the sixty-fifth session of the UN General Assembly, awarded the coordinator of the UNDP Regional HIV Program in the Arab States, a Tunisian woman, Khadija Moalla, the 3rd Annual Global South-South Development Award for the CHAHAMA initiative (Network of Multi-Faith-Based Organizations in response to HIV) (Moalla, 2012: 24). The award reflected the fact that the principles of the Cairo Declaration were introduced throughout the Arab region, at community, national, subregional, and regional levels. The overall aim of CHAHAMA was to bring "together the hundreds of Christian, Muslim, female and male religious leaders in the Arab region who have been mobilized, trained and are making a difference in the AIDS response from community to regional level." (Faith-Based Organizations at the Forefront in the AIDS Response in the Arab Region, 2012)

Conclusion

> What we have stumbled upon through the MDGs is the com-
> mon currency of development...so we share the determina-
> tion to ensure that this framework is supported by all of us
> as we move beyond 2015. (Olav Kjörven, deputy administra-
> tor of UNDP and director of the Bureau for Development
> Policy; http://www.unfpa.org/webdav/site/global/shared
> /documents/news/2012/UN-FBO%20Roundtable%20
> MDGs%20Beyond%202015%20Report%202.pdf)

There was a mixed outcome in relation to international
development at the UN, involving FBOs. Regarding two specific issues, captured in two of the MDGs—"Promote gender
equality and empower women" and "Combat HIV/AIDS,
malaria and other diseases"—there was progress, centering on
development of UN agency/faith networks, involving, in the
case studies, UNFPA and UNDP. Each worked with separate
groups of religious leaders and FBOs with a shared aim: to
develop specific campaigns and foci to collect and disseminate
human and material resources to pursue specific development-
oriented goals. We also noted the failure of the World Bank-
WCC initiative that eventually came to nothing, despite a
promising start. Part of the reason for this was their mutual
ideological incompatibility, which made continued progress in
their relationship impossible to achieve.

6
Human Rights and "Defamation of Religion"

> United Nations resolutions on the "defamation of religions" are incompatible with the fundamental freedoms of individuals to freely exercise and peacefully express their thoughts, ideas, and beliefs. (What is "defamation of religion"; http://whatisdefamationofreligion.wordpress.com/)

> Since 1999, several non-binding resolutions have been voted on and accepted by the UN condemning "defamation of religion." The motions, sponsored on behalf of the Organization of the Islamic Conference, aim to prohibit expression that would "fuel discrimination, extremism and misperception leading to polarization and fragmentation with dangerous unintended and unforeseen consequences." Religious groups, human rights activists, free-speech activists, and several countries in the West have condemned the resolutions arguing it amounts to an international blasphemy law. (Dacey, 2012)

As this book has shown, faith-linked issues "returned" to international relations following the end of the Cold War. Fifteen years ago, a lengthy (72 pp.) report, "Religion Counts. Religion and Public Policy at the UN" (2002: x), noted that there was "clearly an increased religious presence at the UN."[1] From the early 1990s, Bush (2005: 5) claims, "religious groups have been adopting increasingly assertive stances at the UN." Today, more than 300 FBOs engage with the UN in various ways and for sundry reasons. Overall, it is clear that now there are only numerous faith-linked groups at the UN but also what they do there is pursued in many cases with vigor and persistence (Carrette and Trigeaud, 2013). The nature and consequences of FBO involvement at the UN have so far been examined empirically in chapters 4 and 5. In chapter 4, we focused on sexual and reproductive health rights and, in chapter 5, international development in the context of the MDGs. We saw that in both cases FBOs were not united on these issues and there was no generic faith position to contrast with a common secular approach to these issues. Instead, the issues split not only FBOs but also UN actors along ideological lines.

The current chapter completes the trio of empirically focused chapters in looking at a further, highly divisive topic, defamation of religion. This issue has polarized FBO opinion at the UN over the last 15 years, and continues to be a major unresolved bone of contention. It divides those who believe that it is unacceptable to critique religion from those who aver that a (secular) human right—the right of freedom of expression—is most important, a sentiment expressed in the first quotation above. The second quotation notes that, since its introduction in 1999, the focal point of the defamation of religion campaign has been the 57-member Organization of Islamic Cooperation (OIC), operating in tandem with several non-Islamic actors. Critics aver that the OIC-led campaign is actually designed to protect just one religion—Islam—in order to enable governments in some Muslim-majority countries, such as Pakistan and Sudan, to malign and/or mistreat their religious minorities with impunity.

The issue emerged at the UN in the late 1990s, and was subsequently given a major fillip by several important international events. These included the events of September 11, 2001; the subsequent "war on terror," including the invasions of Afghanistan (2001) and Iraq (2003), spearheaded by the government of the United States; the so-called "Danish cartoons" controversy following the publication of denigratory cartoons in the *Jyllands-Posten* newspaper (2005); the online "release" of a 2012 film, *Innocence of Muslims*, which, like the *Jyllands-Posten* cartoons, outraged many Muslims by depicting Prophet Mohammed in a very unfavorable light; and, finally, also in 2012, the appearance of further cartoons that poked fun at Prophet Mohammed in the French satirical weekly magazine, *Charlie Hebdo* (Beittinger-Lee and Miall, 2012). In addition, there was a continuing focus on the treatment of Muslims in Europe in the context of a resurgence of far-right political parties, including the *Front National* (France) and the Freedom Party (Austria), both of which did well in elections to the European parliament in 2014. Overall, the enduring, yet unresolved, defamation of religion controversy reflects three key points:

▸ The UN is capable of addressing (although not easily resolving) a highly charged issue that centers on the relationship between faith and human rights;

▸ The system of individually based human rights, whose roots lie in the Western Judaeo-Christian tradition, is regarded by one set of actors at the UN as more important than the right of religion not to be critiqued, a view held by another group;

▸ Safeguarding of minority rights—of Muslims, Christians, and some other minority faith groups, such as Bahá'ís—remains a highly contentious issue at the UN. (Carrette and Miall, 2013: 39)

This chapter traces the development of the defamation of religion controversy at the UN since the late 1990s. The chapter does this in the following way. First, we examine the issue of human rights interpretation internationally after the Cold War in order to contextualize the defamation of religion issue. Second, we focus on the role of the OIC in leading the campaign at the UN to outlaw defamation of religions. The third section of the chapter examines the impact of the most recent (2012) defamation of religion controversies at the UN—the film, *Innocence of Muslims*, and *Charlie Hebdo* cartoons—which reignited the controversy and put the issue squarely back onto the UN agenda.

Human rights after the Cold War

Human rights were emphasized following the end of the Cold War and the contemporaneous deepening of globalization (Ball and Gready, 2006). Three particular aspects of globalization helped focus attention on human rights at this time:

▸ *Collapse of communist governments in central and eastern Europe.* In the name of fighting communism during the Cold War, Western governments turned a blind eye to non-democratic allies' often poor human rights records. Once communism in central and eastern Europe was "defeated," however, Western pressure increased on human rights abusing governments, including allies.
▸ *Growth of transnational human rights organizations.* Cross-border campaigning organizations, such as Amnesty

International and Human Rights Watch, worked interactively with domestic civil society groups. Together they encouraged human rights violating governments to reform and adopt international human rights norms and regimes.

▶ The post–Cold War focus on human rights reflected a rediscovered universalism, a trend that also appeared after World War II, exemplified in the creation of the UN. President George H. W. Bush proclaimed a "New World Order," followed soon after by "progressive globalization" rhetoric of UK prime minister Tony Blair and US president George W. Bush.

The overall impact of these developments was to highlight Western governments' expressions of support for interlinked universalist goals after the Cold War: improved human rights in poor countries, including better social justice, more democracy, and improved development, especially for those who most egregiously lacked these goods, including, in many cases, poor women and religious minorities. Consequently, both Western governments and IGOs—notably, the European Union—as well as several influential UN agencies, such as the World Bank and the International Monetary Fund—became more assertive in demanding human rights improvements. Their demands were often articulated in the rhetoric of "political conditionality," designed to test human rights observance in relation to the granting or withholding of external development assistance (Haynes, 2002). Finally, transnational human rights entities—including Amnesty International, Human Rights Watch, and Freedom House—also became more vocal and visible in seeking to monitor governments' observance of human rights norms. According to Pridham (2000: 295), their influence increased as a result of "various developments arising from the rise of new technology and its growth in global connections." Risse (2000) notes the particularly important spread of television, radio and Western-style education as important components of growing international concern with human rights. As a result, "any country's claim that the way it treats its subjects is no one else's business has now become a relic of a past age" (Bealey, 1999: 141).

Despite international concern, the 1990s were marked by emergence of new human rights issues which became focal points of international concern, concerning inappropriate treatment by governments of ethnic and/or religious communities minorities in, *inter alia*, Sudan, Rwanda, and Iran (Harrop and Hague, 2001; Webber and Smith, 2002). Contemporaneously, the international community was vocal in support of post-conflict war-crime tribunals in relation to the Gulf War (1990–1991), Rwanda (1994), Sierra Leone (mid-1990s–2002), former Yugoslavia (1993–2001), and Iraq (2003) (Puddington, 2007).

Defamation of religion and the OIC

The OIC-led campaign against defamation of religion reflected wide-ranging international concern with human rights after the Cold War. Following its introduction in 1999, the OIC-led campaign was initially tolerated or even supported—albeit often in a rather desultory fashion—by many governments and non-state actors at the UN. Over time, however, it became apparent to many governments, NGOs, and FBOs, with a consequent waning of support, that a person could be executed for defamation of religion in an OIC-member state, such as Pakistan. How did this square with an emerging and enlarging universalist human rights regime, they asked? When it became clear that there was no easy or simple answer to this question, the UN became the key global battleground for subsequent disagreements about a key "human right": the right to denigrate religions in the context of freedom of expression, a cornerstone of human rights, expressed in the UN Charter. After a dozen years of rankling about the issue, the UN officially recognized the human right to blaspheme in September 2011 (General Comment No. 34; http://www2.ohchr.org/english/bodies/hrc/docs/GC34.pdf). This appeared to reflect the triumph of the human rights view over the defamation of religion approach at the UN, although as we shall see below that this did not resolve the matter.

The background of the UN—reflected, for example, in the 1948 Human Rights Charter—is emphatically in individually orientated human rights. Carrette and Miall (2013: 39) note that "individually based universal human rights" take precedence at the UN, reflecting the organization's "Western Judaeo-Christian tradition." Regarding FBOs, we have already noted that north-based Christian FBOs are overrepresented at the UN, in terms of numbers of Christians in the world, in relation to members of other faiths from other regions. Other world religions, with the exception of Judaism, are significantly underrepresented in terms of numbers of FBOs at the UN compared to the overall numbers of followers of those faiths. This is especially clear in relation to the world's second largest faith, Islam. According to Carrette and Miall (2013: 20), "more than 70% of 'religious' NGOs identified themselves as Christian" at the UN, while around 50 (that is, one-sixth) are "Islamic." Although the number of Islamic FBOs at the UN is slowly growing, those with official consultative status at the UN in 2013 were still very few compared to north-based Christian FBOs.

Despite the relatively small number of Muslim FBOs at the UN, David Littman (1999) asserts that Islam's international influence and involvement is increasing, with "Islamism grow[ing] stronger at the United Nations." Littman's reference to "Islamism" at the UN appears to be primarily an assertion related to increasing Muslim-majority *governmental* activity, in terms both of individual countries and FBOs strongly linked to individual states, such as the Muslim World League, organized and financed from Saudi Arabia. At the UN, the OIC is the key Islamic FBO, by virtue of its size, clout, and institutional position. This is not however to imply that OIC member states form a cohesive bloc based on their shared Islamic faith, not least because the Islamic world is significantly divided between Sunni and Shia interpretations of Islam. In addition, the OIC functions primarily as an interstate organization, although the existence of several specialist agencies, not run by individual member governments, also emphasizes the wide-ranging focus of the OIC at the UN.

The OIC was established in 1969. The organization's proclaimed *raison d'être* is to be "the collective voice of the Muslim world," working to pursue "international peace and harmony among various people of the world." (http://www.oic-oci.org/page_detail.asp?p_id=52). Over the last four decades, the OIC has functioned as a forum for senior Muslim figures to discuss faith-linked issues in international relations, while also consistently asserting the desirability of a path of moderation in relation to world affairs (Ahsan, 1988). While the OIC's overall role in international relations has not been widely debated, many observers would probably agree that it has been relatively insignificant (Akbarzadeh and Connor, 2004; Esposito, 2002; Kepel, 2004; Roy, 2004). A key reason for this is that while the OIC professes to be the primary voice of the *ummah*, working to extend the global growth and influence of Islam, it has instead been dogged for decades by competition between leading member states, including Egypt, Iran, Pakistan, Turkey, and Saudi Arabia (Haynes, 2001). Dogan avers that *if* the OIC could overcome interstate rivalry, it would be more than capable of helping Muslims and Muslim states to pull together to deliver

> a unified ethical approach to such issues as international terrorism, international development, and democracy. In addition, the global role of the OIC is seen to be potentially critical for ending both 'clashes' between 'civilizations' and bringing peace to the 'Greater Middle East.'

(Dogan, 2005: 1)

From the late 1990s, OIC activities at the UN focused on highlighting the desirability of establishing binding international conventions concerning defamation of religion. The campaign was controversial for two main reasons. First, as we have already noted, the UN is a liberal secular organization whose creation and development after World War II emphasized and exemplified the decidedly secular turn in international relations from the mid-seventeenth century, following the end of Europe's inter-Christian religious wars. Yet, although the UN is strongly secular in orientation, many of its member states actually represent communities comprising a majority of people with faith beliefs. Kuru (2009) estimates that of 197 extant countries in the world (the UN has 193 member states), nearly two-thirds (117) are officially secular nations, while five (Cuba, North Korea, Cambodia, Vietnam, and Laos) are "Communist anti-religious" states. Kuru also identifies 12 "religious states," 11 of which have Muslim-majority populations, while the twelfth is the Holy See (The Vatican), the only non-Muslim religious state.[2] In addition, according to Kuru, nearly one-third of UN member states—that is, 60 countries—have an established religion. Note, however, that to have an established religion does not necessarily imply that faith has a consistently important public role. For example, the United Kingdom, Norway (until recently), and Iceland all have established churches—respectively, the Anglican Church, the Church of Norway, and the Evangelical Lutheran Church of Iceland—yet each is a secular country. Fifteen Muslim-majority states have Islam as their established religion, and some of them have *Sharia* law as their primary legislative source.[3] In addition, Kuru identifies another 20 Muslim-majority countries that are officially secular, that is, where no religion is officially privileged over others (Kuru, 2009: 247–253).[4] On the other hand, Kayaoğlu (2011: 7) notes that

> while differences exist among the non-secular Muslim-majority states as well as between them and the secular Muslim-majority states, these states sometimes overcome their differences and present a formidable bloc within the UN. As in the Danish Cartoon Crisis, these states *have increasingly brought Muslim agendas, grievances, and demands to the UN.* (emphasis added)

The "formidable bloc" of Muslim countries has an organizational focal point: the OIC, notable for setting and pursuing "Muslim agendas, grievances, and demands," including in relation to trying to achieve a binding UN resolution on defamation of religion. Over time, the measure, initially supported by many UN members, including some non-Muslim-majority countries, became highly controversial. No consensual agreement was achieved. As debates and discussed proceeded, defamation of religion developed into an increasingly polarized confrontation involving, on one side, the OIC, some governments of Muslim-majority countries, and an important umbrella group of some 36 Muslim FBOs, the Muslim World League (or *Rabita* from *Rabita al-Alam al-Islami*). The Muslim World League (MWL) is a group of Islamic FBOs. It is one of the largest Islamic FBOs, with 36 constituent offices around the world. MWL has offices in London, and, in the United States, in New York and Washington, as well as 10 "external centers" in Europe, and 10 "external offices" in Africa and the Middle East (http://www.discoverthenetworks.org/printgroupProfile. asp?grpid=7347).

The MWL was founded in 1962 by *ulama* (Islamic religious figures) from 22 countries, with headquarters in Mecca, Saudi Arabia. Since its inception it has been funded by the government of Saudi Arabia. According to its website, the League

> is engaged in propagating the religion of Islam, elucidating its principles and tenets, refuting suspicious and false allegations made against the religion. The League also strives to persuade people to abide by the commandments of their Lord, and to keep away from prohibited deeds. The League is also ready to help Muslims solve problems facing them anywhere in the world, and carry out their projects in the sphere of Da'wa [that is, to invite or summon someone], education and culture. The League, which employs all means that are not at variance with the Sharia (Islamic law) to further its aims, is well known for rejecting all acts of violence and promoting dialogue with the people of other cultures. (http://www. themwl.org/Profile/default.aspx?l=EN)

At the time of its founding, MWL's *raison d'être* was as a faith-based, non-state, counter-initiative opposed to the then influential secular Arab nationalism, led and directed by Egypt's then president, Gamal Abdul Nasser. MWL is associated with promotion of a strict Wahhabi brand of Islam, of the kind that is state policy in Saudi Arabia, although it also broadens its reach by teaming up with other Islamic FBOs, including the Muslim Brotherhood ("Muslim World League Meeting Includes U.S. and European Muslim Brotherhood," 2014). At the OIC, the MWL has observer status, enabling the league to attend all OIC meetings and conferences, and is also a member of OIC's Islamic Educational, Scientific and Cultural Organization (ISESCO). MWL is affiliated to the UN, enjoying consultative status with ECOSOC, as well as being associated with the United Nations Children's Fund (UNICEF) and the United Nations Educational, Scientific and Cultural Organization (UNESCO). After the 9/11 attacks, US federal agents raided MWL's US offices and later Abdurahman Alamoudi, who worked for the League, was convicted of sending funds to terrorist groups and ordered to serve 23 years in prison (El-Menshawy, 2004).

The global organization and reach of the MWL is particularly important in the context of there being relatively few Islamic FBOs at the UN. Apart from MWL, which has a wide-ranging focus as reflected in the quotation above, most FBOs at the UN, including Islamic Relief and the Washington, DC-based, *Salam* Institute for Peace and Justice, have narrower developmental, humanitarian or interfaith dialogue/peace building foci (Bouta, 2005). In other words, there is no cohesive approach or focus linking most of the 50 or so Islamic FBOs registered with ECOSOC at the UN and MWL stands out for the size of its network and organizational capacity. Linking up with the OIC, MWL was an important component of the wider OIC-led campaign against defamation of religion. It is necessary to make clear, however, that unlike what some scholars claim (e.g., Larsen, 2014), the defamation of religion campaign was not solely an Islamic campaign; instead, the OIC led the campaign that also included non-Islamic actors, such as the Russian Orthodox Church and the government of Russia, and the government of (atheist) China.

The OIC-led campaign was strongly opposed by the European Union, most Western states—including the Holy See—as well as many NGOs and some FBOs (Larsen, 2014). The key bone of contention was the issue of human rights *versus* those of religion not to be insulted or defamed. The OIC-led campaign was seen by many secular NGOs and Western governments, as well as by numerous Christian and Jewish FBOs and some Muslim FBOs, to be primarily a self-interested fight not only to privilege Islam over other faiths but also to cover up the fact that in some Muslim countries, like Pakistan and Sudan, a person can be executed for "defaming" Islam by, for example, seeking to convert to a different faith. In addition, critics believed that, if adopted, defamation of religion would be used to make life harder for already besieged religious minorities in some Muslim countries, such as Ahmadis and Bahá'ís. Finally, opponents of the defamation of religion initiative averred that, if adopted, the measure would likely be used in some Muslim-majority countries to prevent non-Muslim missionaries from proselytizing there.

Under the leadership of the OIC, the campaign crystallized in a series of resolutions at the UN. The starting point was to aver that justification for the defamation of religion measure was not new: instead, it was already existing in various UN human rights documents that, the campaign contended, made combating defamation of religion a necessary goal of the UN. Consequently, so the argument went, governments around the world were duty bound to take steps in support of the campaign. The argument was that, following September 11, 2001, and attendant talk about conflict between civilizations (Huntington, 1993; 1996), there were strong reasons to increase interfaith dialogue and tolerance, and the defamation of religions measure was a necessary step forward. That is, if there was a strong measure to make religious hate speech unacceptable then there was said to be a greater chance to developing civilizational coexistence. While the plea was that governments should make all necessary efforts to combat defamation of religions, it was by no means clear what this measure would practically imply. Would it mean curtailing free speech, as opponents of the measure claimed?

The government of Pakistan introduced a draft resolution in 1999 at the UN against defamation of religion. It was not accepted by the general assembly. Critics, including the governments of Germany (representing the EU), Canada, and Norway, each of which proposed significant amendments to the draft, pointed to what they saw as language that was too "religious" and partisan (Kayaoğlu, 2011: 22). While this did not amount to outright rejection of the proposed measure *per se*, it did highlight a growing ideological polarization on the issue at the UN between advocates and opponents of the measure. This did not prevent, in 2005, the UN's Human Rights Commission (replaced in 2006 by the Human Rights Council [HRC])[5] and the General Assembly from accepting a resolution entitled, "Combating Defamation of Religions" ("United Nations Documentation: Research Guide," n/d). Five years later, in March 2010, Pakistan's government—acting on behalf of the OIC—put forward a further draft resolution to the HRC. It sought to proscribe activity that would "fuel discrimination, extremism and misperception leading to polarization and fragmentation with dangerous unintended and unforeseen consequences" (Human Rights Council, 2010: 3).

Pakistan's 2010 draft resolution to the HRC did not get the necessary support. By this time, it was clear that defamation of religion was an issue that, perhaps more than any other, polarized opinion between the OIC, individual Muslim governments, significant Muslim FBOs, including the Muslim World League, the Russian Orthodox Church, and the governments of Russia and China. Opposing this multi-faith and multicultural coalition was a group of states and non-state actors opposed to the measure. This group included some FBOs, as well as human rights and free-speech activists, who shared the view that freedom of expression was more important than proscribing defamation of religions. According to Tiffany Barrans of the US-based "Evangelical Law Firm," the American Center for Law and Justice, "All nations that respect religious freedom and freedom of expression should take a strong stance against any push for a defamations-of-religions resolution." This is because, she argued, "a person's right to freedom of expression, even expression that might be deemed offensive, is considered a 'cornerstone right,' without which other rights fall into jeopardy." (Goodenough, 2012; also see Trangerud, 2014)

Barrans is arguing that the concept of defamation of religion conflicts with a universal human right that, its proponents argue, must take precedence over efforts to protect faiths from criticism or attack. This right is freedom of thought, conscience, and faith itself—which builds on the principle that to designate certain ideas to be beyond debate and discussion by believers and nonbelievers alike is unacceptable. The point is that even though it may well be

> deeply hurtful and offensive to have another person criticize your religious beliefs, this is not in and of itself a violation of your rights, and you are free to mount a defense with a speech of your own. By contrast, restricting such speech is a violation of the right to free expression, codified in Article 19 of International Covenant on Civil and Human Rights.[6]
>
> (Goodenough, 2012)

Critics of the proposed defamation of religions measure also argued that in some countries, laws against defamation of religions have been used to repress religious minorities, to restrict the ability of members of the majority religious community to practice their faith in the way they choose, and even to settle personal grudges. For example, in Pakistan in 2012, Radsch reports, 16 people were awaiting execution for blasphemy, while 20 more were serving life sentences in prison for the same offence. In addition, a 14-year-old Christian girl with mental disabilities was arrested in Pakistan in August 2012 for allegedly desecrating a Qur'an. A year earlier, two prominent Pakistani politicians were assassinated merely for advocating reform of Pakistan's blasphemy law to allow equal treatment for other extant faiths in the country, including Hinduism and Christianity, the two largest minority faiths. Finally, in Egypt in September 2012, a 24-year-old activist was charged with blasphemy after sharing scenes on Facebook from the controversial film, *Innocence of Muslims* and speaking negatively about Islam (Radsch, 2012).

Reflecting such concerns, the US-based NGO Freedom House produced a special report in 2010, titled "Policing Belief: the Impact of Blasphemy Laws on Human Rights." The focus of the report is on human rights implications of domestic blasphemy and religious insult laws. Seven countries are examined in the report: Algeria, Egypt, Greece, Indonesia, Malaysia, Pakistan, and Poland. In each country, anti-blasphemy laws exist both on paper and in practice. The report finds that in each of the countries, anti-blasphemy laws violate a fundamental freedom: that of expression. This is because the anti-blasphemy laws are by definition designed to protect one particular class of actor: faith leaders and institutions, and related doctrine, from insult or offence. Even when relatively benign, the report found that the existence of such a law tended to encourage self-censorship. For example, in two democratic countries focused upon in the report, Greece and Poland, charges were brought against entertainers and intellectuals—including high-profile artists, curators, and writers—in order to warn others to avoid certain topics if they wished to escape prosecution. In both Pakistan and Malaysia, on the other hand, similar laws were discovered to lead to overt governmental censorship, with violators sent to prison for long periods of time. In sum, according to Freedom House, "there is no evidence that restricting speech reduces religious intolerance. In fact, the evidence shows that prohibitions on blasphemy actually encourage or justify intolerance and lead to a wide range of human rights abuses, including religious discrimination, arbitrary arrest, torture, and even murder"(Radsch, 2012; also see Freedom House, 2010).

The concerns expressed by Freedom House were similar to those held by other opponents of the proposed defamation of religion. Critics condemned the pro-defamation of religion campaign as *de facto* an unwelcome attempt to impose a generalized, international blasphemy law, to which they were fundamentally opposed. In addition, critics of the pro-defamation of religion campaign argued that, while masquerading as a human rights measure, it was actually a highly politicized attempt to strengthen domestic anti-blasphemy and religious defamation laws that would primarily benefit authoritarian governments in some Muslim-majority countries. If introduced, critics contended, the laws were likely to be used unjustifiably to punish those expressing antigovernment opinions in Muslim countries, including journalists, students, and other peaceful political dissidents. In addition, critics noted that the resolution, championed by governments of countries with existing blasphemy laws, including Iran, Pakistan, and Egypt, might use the measure further to target already vulnerable religious minorities, including Shias and members of the Ahmadiyya sect in Pakistan,[7] Bahá'ís in Iran, and Christian Copts in Egypt (Fox, 2008). In other words, the fear was that religious minorities with different views to majority religions—including, Sunni Islam in Pakistan and Egypt and Shia Islam in Iran—might well be persecuted under cover of defamation of religion.

Over time, the antireligious defamation campaign acquired growing support to the extent that in April 2011, it came to an unsuccessful, albeit temporary, end at the UN. At this time, proponents of the measure accepted that, as result of opposition, it was impossible to get UN General Assembly agreement to a binding measure on defamation of religion. It was clear that the controversy had gone beyond defamation of religion *tout court*—to become symptomatic of a more general normative polarization at the UN on the relationship of faith and human rights. On the one hand, there was the pro-defamation of religion bloc, bringing together governments of Muslim-majority countries and Islamic FBOs, notably the Muslim World League, plus non-Islamic allies, including the Russian Orthodox Church and the governments of Russia and China. On the other hand, there was a collective of non-state and state actors sharing a pro–human rights approach, reflecting shared liberal views, including governments of west European governments, the EU, many secular NGOs, and some FBOs. What this group had in common was adhesion to the notion of freedom of speech and of expression. Overall, it is clear that the controversial issue was a severe test for the UN and its liberal-secular preference when seeking to accommodate the views of some faiths.

The issue also highlights a point I have made earlier in this book. That is, the OIC-led campaign did not rely on faith arguments to pursue its objectives. That is, despite clearly being a faith issue, the defamation of religion campaign did not rely on faith-based arguments to make its case, instead preferring to use arguments based on secular liberal principles that the OIC probably believed were more likely to find favor at the UN. The OIC and allies found it necessary to accept liberal-secular groups'

> prerogative in defining the meaning, scope, and applicability of these categories. In other words, the liberal golden strait-jacket allowed Islamic voices to translate their argument into an acceptable language, but it also made them vulnerable to liberal groups' counter-claims on terminology. In this discur-sive conflict the liberals had the upper hand in deciding what key terms actually meant. Thus liberals continued to chal-lenge the Islamic actors regarding the precise definitions of "defamation," "race," and "right" and questioned the necessity and feasibility of anti-defamation norms within international human rights. In all these interactions, liberal-secular groups largely avoided discussing the Islamic demands: combating Islamophobia can be a means of protecting Muslims' rights in the West. (Kayaoğlu, 2011: 20)

Kayaoğlu's point gains credence when we note the array of opposition to the defamation of religion measure, including from a (perhaps) surprisingly large number of FBOs. Among the measure's most vocal opponents were a collection of NGOs and FBOs from various backgrounds and traditions. By June 2014, representatives of 239 NGOs and FBOs had signed a motion at the "UN Watch" website, expressing deep concern at the

> pervasive and mounting campaign by the Organization of the Islamic Conference (OIC) to produce UN resolutions, declarations, and world conferences that propagate the con-cept of defamation of religions, a concept having no basis in domestic or international law, and *that would alter the very meaning of human rights, which protect individuals from harm, but not beliefs from critical inquiry* (emphasis added; UN Watch Press Release, 2009).

Various FBOs—including from Muslim, Christian, and Jewish faith backgrounds—signed a relevant "UN Watch" motion.[8] Among Islamic FBOs that signed the petition were the Muslim Council of Canada, Ahmadiyya Muslim Community, Muslims against Sharia, Council of ex-Muslims of Britain, Coalition for Defence of Human Rights in the Muslim World, American Islamic Congress, and American Islamic Forum for Democracy. Christian FBO signatories included Christian Solidarity Worldwide, International Christian Concern, All India Christian Council, and Middle East Christian Committee. From the Jewish faith, petition signers comprised World Jewish Congress, European Union of Jewish Students, International Council of Jewish Women, American Jewish Congress, Consultative Council of Jewish Organizations, World Union of Jewish Students, and Jewish Human Rights Coalition (UK). In addition, eight NGOs—none of which were signatories to the UN Watch petition—submitted opinions to the Human Rights Council; and seven of them strongly opposed the resolution. Included among the seven were Christian evangelical organizations (such as, the American Center for Law and Justice (ACLJ), with an active "international affiliate," the European Center for Law and Justice, a "Christian-inspired" FBO with special consultative status with ECOSOC since 2007), a humanist entity (International Humanist and Ethical Union [IHEU]), and three liberal human rights organizations (International Center against Censorship, Becket Fund for Religious Liberty, and Cairo Institute for Human Rights Studies). The IHEU called the resolution a *jihad* on free speech. Several NGOs, brought together by the American Jewish Congress formed an advocacy network, the Coalition to Defend Free Speech, specifically to oppose the resolution (The Coalition to Defend Free Speech, 2008). The overall thrust of these attacks from both faith and secular perspectives was to proclaim that the OIC-led campaign against defamation of religion was in reality a generalized global attack on free speech designed primarily to (1) protect the Islamic faith against critique, and (2) enable governments of some Muslim-majority countries to persecute non-Muslims in their countries under the guise of preventing or punishing defamation of religion.

In April 2011, the result of a dozen years of opposition to the OIC-led campaign to incorporate a wide-ranging defamation of religions measure (temporarily) ended. Over time, it became increasingly clear that the issue polarized both governments and non-state actors, both secular and faith-based, at the UN. This is because the measure was seen by growing numbers of critics to represent a cynical attempt by the OIC and its allies to introduce and disseminate a self-interested measure. The argument was that, while ostensibly in place to try to deal with religious hate-speech and improve inter-civilizational relations, introduction of the measure would likely facilitate attempts by governments of some Muslim countries—those pointed to in this regard included Pakistan, Iran, and Egypt—who might use the measure as an opportunity to persecute already-vulnerable religious minorities including, respectively, Ahmadis, Bahá'ís, and Coptic Christians, as well as to stifle freedom of speech and legitimate political opposition against incumbent governments. In sum, for more than a decade from 1999, the OIC led a campaign called for the outlawing of religious defamation, pushing through resolutions at the UN General Assembly and Human Rights Council each year. Western democracies and a variety of secular and faith-based non-state entities opposed the move and, in April 2011, the OIC suspended its campaign.

New "defamation of religion" controversies: *Innocence of Muslims* and *Charlie Hebdo* cartoons

The temporary end of the OIC-led campaign was a pragmatic response to a deal made with the Obama administration. In

March 2011, the US government and the OIC cosponsored a compromise resolution at the UN condemning "stigmatization" based on religion but differing from the earlier "defamation measures by not calling for legal restrictions—except in the specific case of religion-based 'incitement to imminent violence.'" (Goodenough, 2011) However, while the US government saw the resolution as a breakthrough after years of increasingly polarized debate at the UN, this was not the end of the matter.

Following the agreement with the government of the United States, the OIC did not put forward its annual defamation of religion resolution in 2011. Instead, both supporters and critics off the proposed measure agreed to replace it with Human Rights Council Resolution 16/18, titled "Combating Intolerance, Negative Stereotyping and Stigmatization of, and Discrimination, Incitement to Violence and Violence Against, Persons Based on Religion or Belief" (http://www.ohchr.org/ Documents/Issues/Religion/AdditionalInfoSGReport67_178. pdf). The resolution focused on the rights of individuals to be free from intolerance and discrimination based on religion while also calling upon states to take concrete steps to protect religious freedom, prohibit discrimination and hate crimes, and counter offensive expression through dialogue, education, and public debate rather than criminalization of speech.

Both OIC member states and Western governments, including that of the United States, supported HRC Resolution 16/18 when it was introduced. Following the resolution, a follow up—the Istanbul Process—was launched, which focused on how governments could actually implement recommendations in the resolution. Over the next two years, expert-level meetings took place (in the United States in 2011 and in the

United Kingdom in December 2012) (http://www.mfa.gov.tr/
istanbul-process-on-regional-security-and-cooperation-for-a-
secure-and-stable-afghanistan.en.mfa).

However, if the Obama administration hoped that the
compromise agreement would defuse the issue and eventu-
ally make it go away, it was to be disappointed. Intense
controversy about defamation of religions reappeared soon
after the Istanbul Process was inaugurated. This was a consequence in 2012 of (1) the internet release of a 74-minute
film, *Innocence of Muslims*, and (2) cartoons depicting Prophet
Mohammed unfavorably published by a French satirical
magazine, *Charlie Hebdo*. The release of the film *Innocence of
Muslims* by an extreme anti-Muslim Egyptian Christian cam-
paigner in the United States sparked fury among Muslims
and resulted in the killing of the US ambassador to Libya and
three other embassy officials in an attack in Benghazi in July
2012. More than 50 people died in deadly protests throughout
the Muslim world as protesters engaged in clashes with the
police. In Egypt, Libya, and Yemen protesters stormed US
embassies and consulates. As Tiffany Barrans, International
Legal Director of ACLJ, noted: "In light of the recent demon-
strations and attacks in the name of Allah, it is likely that the
United Nations will see a renewed push for a defamation of
religions resolution." (Goodenough, 2012)

Following the film's appearance on the internet and associated violence and deaths in Egypt, Libya, and Yemen, President
Obama addressed the UN General Assembly in September
2012. Obama condemned the film but declined to ban it as to
do so would violate the first amendment to the US constitution
that guarantees freedom of expression by prohibiting Congress
from restricting the press or the rights of individuals to speak
freely.[9] Following Obama's statement, Turkey's prime minister,

Recep Tayyip Erdoğan, declared himself disappointed with what he called Obama's "soft" response to the appearance of the film. Erdoğan said he was "saddened" by the attitude of Obama, mentioning a telephone conversation he had with the US president, who claimed that defamation targeting Christians can also be provocative but is evaluated within the scope of "freedom of expression." This seemed to imply that, for Obama, "freedom" to denigrate religions was more important than restricting free speech. Meanwhile, Erdoğan mentioned that the Ankara 13th Criminal Court of Peace has already ruled to ban the film from broadcasting in Turkey and to block access to it via the Internet. He clearly stated the resolute stance of the Turkish Ministry of Transportation, Maritime Affairs and Communication to prevent the distribution of the film in Turkey.

Delivering a message to the international community on the necessity of introducing a mechanism that would protect sacred values from insult, Erdoğan mentioned Obama's positive assessment of such a mechanism. However, he claimed that he was expecting a harsher reaction to the film from the US president.

Obama's moderate response to the film also seemed to elicit a reaction from Egyptian president Mohammed Morsi. Delivering his first speech before the UN during the sixty-seventh General Assembly in New York, he appeared to be responding to Obama's speech on Tuesday as part of the same meeting, in which the US leader again condemned the video but sternly defended the right to free speech guaranteed by the US Constitution ("Erdoğan 'Saddened' by Obama's Refusal to Ban Anti-Islam Movie," 2012).

A French satirical magazine then chose to add to the debate between freedom of expression and religious defamation when, following the eruption of the global controversy about *Innocence of Muslims*, the magazine, *Charlie Hebdo*, published several cartoons featuring a figure resembling Prophet Mohammed. Stephane Charbonnier, director of the French magazine, said his staff was "not really fuelling the fire" but rather using its freedom of expression "to comment (on) the news in a satirical way" (Bittermann, Meilhan, and Yan, 2012).

The film *Innocence of Muslims* film and the *Charlie Hebdo* cartoons together put pressure on the constituents of the Istanbul Process discussions to try to achieve progress. By 2013, however, it was clear that the process was in trouble. Theoretically, the meetings stemming from the Istanbul Process would offer a new opportunity to direct the world's attention back toward a response to intolerance that does not violate human rights or obstruct the free exchange of ideas (Radsch, 2012). In June 2013, Ambassador Michael G. Kozik, acting principal deputy assistant secretary for Democracy, Human Rights and Labor, expressed the US government's frustration with lack of progress. For Kozik, the Istanbul Process debates were a rerun or continuation of what had been aired at the UN for years in the defamation of religion issue. For Kozik

the narrative [is] in terms reminiscent of the Cold War pits "the West" against "the rest." Religious intolerance throughout the world is attributed to the failure of the West to either endorse or enforce more sweeping criminal prohibitions on speech. It is never explained how prohibiting media in the West from reporting on people who wrongly appropriate to themselves the term "jihadis" would somehow result in better treatment for Christians in Egypt or Shia in Pakistan. Nor is it explained how the application of anti-Semitism laws to anti-Muslim expression would result in better outcomes for Muslims in Europe when we are seeing an increase in anti-Semitism that parallels the growth in anti-Muslim expression—most often from the same groups of haters. Nor is there any examination of why those countries that have expansive restrictions on religious expression also have even higher degrees of religious violence and intolerance than those that do not. (statement by Ambassador Michael G. Kozik, 2013)

Kozik here is expressing a belief widely held among opponents at the UN of the defamation of religion measure. It is presumed by proponents of the measure that getting the "West" to adopt a defamation of religion resolution or achieving

agreement of a broader interpretation of Article 20 of the ICCPR [International Covenant on Civil and Political Rights] than either the Human Rights Committee or the OHCHR [Office of the United Nations High Commissioner for Human Rights] workshops have found warranted would somehow be the silver bullet that fixes all problems.
(statement by Ambassador Michael G. Kozik, 2013)

The question remains whether adoption of the resolution would actually make a real difference in the lives of people throughout the world who are suffering from religious persecution. This, as Fox (2008) makes clear, is a real and growing problem that is beyond the capacity of any government or IGO to resolve.

Conclusion

The current chapter is the third in the book that looks at faith-based controversies at the UN. Chapter 6 examines a highly divisive topic: defamation of religion. Over the last 15 years, the still unresolved issue has polarized opinion at the UN. The topic divides those who believe that it is unacceptable to critique religion (broadly, the "OIC plus allies'" position) from those who aver that a (secular) human right—the right of freedom of expression—is most important (broadly, the West's view). We saw in the chapter that while the issue is often posed as a "OIC *versus* the rest" issue, while the focal point of the defamation of religion campaign is indeed the OIC, it actually brings together a larger "anti-Western" bloc for whom the issue is, in part, an issue of opposing "excessive" "Western" liberalism and/or hegemony. Against this view, critics aver that the OIC-led campaign is actually designed to protect just one faith—Islam—in order to enable governments in some Muslim-majority countries, such as Pakistan and Sudan, to malign and/or mistreat their religious minorities with impunity and to deny the right to proselytize of other faiths. While the defamation of religion campaign was officially put on hold in 2011, two further controversies the following year led to its becoming once again a "hot topic" without achieving resolution.

Overall, the chapter highlights three main conclusions vis-à-vis the activities of FBOs and other actors at the UN in relation to defamation of religion. First, the UN has shown itself capable of addressing a very controversial issue centering on the relationship between faith and human rights. Second, the system of individually based human rights, whose roots lie in the Western Judaeo-Christian tradition, is not universally accepted at the UN as the appropriate set of values in which to assess and deal with defamation of religion issues. Finally, to safeguard faith rights—whether of Muslims in Europe, Christians in Sudan and Egypt, or Bahá'ís in Iran—remains a highly desirable goal that is unfortunately beyond the capacity of the UN to address satisfactorily.

7

Conclusion

The United Nations is

> first and foremost an intergovernmental body
> that owes its existence and is accountable to its
> 192 [now actually 193, following South Sudan's
> entry into the UN in 2011] member states.
>
> (Karam (2012: 23)

Karam's statement implies that the UN's primary
reference point is the collective grouping of world
governments, coming together in the UN General
Assembly. This structure of governance was created after 1945 primarily to give credence to the
UN's overarching human rights mandate, which,
derived from Judaeo-Christian principles in a
secularized format, provides the context to and
explains why the UN provides support to both
governments and civil society actors that pursue
such human rights agendas and goals (Tadjdini,
2013: 36). This Western concept of human rights
gave foundation to the UN. It also explains why
the UN has become a focal point for hundreds of
FBOs that seek the right to be heard and try and

be influential at the UN. There, they pursue human rights and justice objectives in the context of the UN's development. We have also noted the recent and continuing impact of what is noted a as a "widespread religious resurgence" in what is sometimes referred to as postsecular international environment. Together, these topics have formed the subject matter of the book.

Identifiable faith-based organizations at the UN amount to 9–10 percent of the more than 3,700 NGOs registered with the Economic and Social Council (ECOSOC). Approximately two-thirds are Christian and north-based. This does not however imply that they necessarily speak with the same voice, on the same topics, or with the same ideational preferences. This is explained by the fact that, although they share the same nomenclature, there is nevertheless sometimes significant division between strands of the same faith, for example: Christianity (Roman Catholic/Protestant/Orthodox), Islam (Sunni/Shia), Buddhism (Mahayana/Theravada), Judaism (Reform/Orthodox), and Hinduism (numerous gods worshipped). In addition, the great majority of the more than 300 FBOs registered with ECOSOC do not pursue a set of "pure" faith-based concerns to the exclusion of secular interests and goals. Indeed, we have seen that, especially in the case of Christian FBOs, there is very often a thin, blurred, hazy, or even nonexistent dividing line between faith-based and profane concerns.

> One could, as some do, argue that politicized religion is not true religion and what we see happening in the name of religion is nothing more than religious discourse being used to disguise policy choices that in fact contradict "true" religion.
>
> (Tadjdini, 2013: 36)

Whether true or not that this makes it "not true religion"—whatever that is—it seems clear that for many FBOs at the UN there is often no great ideational or value-laden shift necessary to move from a faith-based to a secular worldview and back again. However, what often seems to divide FBOs, sometimes in a quite fundamental way, is the extent to which they are prepared to follow what I have referred to as "politicized" paths to achieve their objectives. That is, to what extent are FBOs prepared to cut deals, be pragmatic, build coalitions, and, in short, use a variety of means to achieve the progress they require to reach their objectives? In this context, many Christian FBOs stand out as willing and able, for the most part, to act in such politicized ways.

As Petersen (2010) notes, FBOs are often motivated by dualistic concerns: on the one hand, "conceptions of a divine justice" and, on the other, faith-influenced people's duty to work for the realization of a goal via, if necessary, worldly methods, tactics, and strategies. This is not however to claim that all FBOs from whatever faith tradition see a similar appropriateness in embarking on politicized campaigns, whether at the UN or more generally. For example, while many Christian FBOs seem to be able to make links between "divine justice and man's duty to work for the realization of this," most Buddhist, Hindu, and Jewish FBOs do not regularly do so, or at least they do not do so regularly at the UN. For example, many of Islamic FBOs active at the UN refer to quotes from the Qur'an as well as sayings and stories of Prophet Mohammed, expressing in faith-based language and from associated contexts, their duty as faith-oriented people, to help those in need. For example, Islamic Relief UK's website contains the following quotation from the Qur'an: "Whoever saved a life, it would be as if they saved the life of all mankind" (Qur'an 5:32). The focus of Islamic Relief UK's work is to respond to "disasters and emergencies" around the world, while promoting "sustainable economic and social development by working with local communities—regardless of race, religion or gender." (http://www.islamic-relief.org.uk/about-us/). Many Jewish FBOs at the UN, on the other hand, have a different modus vivendi. Most were created in the first half of the twentieth century, for a specific purpose: to pursue the goal of a homeland for the Jews, which came into reality with the UN-backed foundation of the state of Israel in 1948. Today, however, Jewish FBOs have a varied relationship with the government of that state.

> While some Jewish NGOs are ambivalent in their relation to the Israeli state and its politics, most do seem to express some degree of sympathy, formulated partly as a support to the country's Palestine policy, partly as a critique of the UN treatment of Israel. *Even the most progressive Jewish NGOs do not directly oppose or criticize the Israeli state.* However, primarily conservative NGOs have entered into cooperation with Israel.
>
> (emphasis added; Petersen, 2010)

This indicates that many Jewish FBOs at the UN, whether characterized as conservative or liberal, still have their roots in the core concern that led to the creation: a homeland for the Jews in the context of their interwar persecution in many European countries. Finally, the handful of Buddhist and Hindu FBOs at the UN, such as the World Fellowship of Buddhists, the Asian Buddhist Conference for Peace, and the Hindu Council of New Zealand, are chiefly active in interfaith dialogue and development contexts and rarely become involved in the kind of politicized campaigns to achieve politicized concerns of the kind we saw in chapters 4–6. In sum, Christian FBOs regularly work in both faith-based and secular contexts, by translating theological precepts into secular foci. The relatively few Muslim, Jewish, Buddhist, and Hindu FBOs at the UN, on the other hand, work in a variety of more constrained ways for goals that seem to chime with faith-based concerns or, in the case of Jewish FBOs, culturally relevant objectives.

As we have noted repeatedly, all FBOs necessarily work within a UN context that is indefatigably liberal and secular, whose concerns, exemplified by the Universal Declaration of Human Rights (1948) and expressed consistently over the years both in the general assembly and in many of the organization's 60 specialist agencies, focus unswervingly on a range of Judaeo-Christian derived, individualistically oriented, justice and human rights goals. I argued in this book that if FBOs want to have a realistic chance of influencing debates and discussions and ultimately affect global public policy outcomes at the UN, they need to both accept and adopt the UN's liberal-secular ethos, code, and modus operandi. This requires them to espouse "appropriate" UN-sanctioned language, concept, and modes of engagement when they work there while engaging in public diplomacy, in networking, and in engaging with UN entities, including the general assembly and dozens of specialized agencies that have developed over the years. To be successful, this requires "translating" faith-based ideas and concepts into secular ones, in order to work in the lingua franca of the UN: secular-liberal concepts and goals.

Chapters 1–3 examined the development of FBOs at the UN, their growth in numbers in the context of both religious resurgence and emergence of postsecular international relations, and theoretical explanations for these changes. Chapters 4–6 shared a common aim: to examine FBO engagement at the UN in relation to three specific controversial issues. Chapter 4 engaged with the topic of (female) sexual and reproductive health rights (SRHR). The issue focuses on a key, highly controversial issue, where conservative FBOs, led and coordinated by the Holy See, square up to, confront, and enter into conflict with liberal entities, including many secular NGOs, some FBOs and a UN agency, the United Nations Population Fund. These conservatives and liberals differ fundamentally from each other in how they understand and interpret a key human rights disagreement: that is, a woman's right to choose *versus* the rights of the unborn child. In addition, at the UN, numerous conservative faith-based and secular entities—both state and non-state actors—focus on related issues too: family policy issues that overlap with feminist concerns, including abortion and the politics of sex and gender. This issue epitomizes the straddling of the intellectual and conceptual division between secular and faith-based, bringing together both conservative and liberal entities at the UN in pursuit of diametrically opposed goals.

In chapter 5 we examined the issue of FBO involvement in human development issues in the context of the MDGs, a *cause célèbre* at the UN since the late 1990s. The issue is generally about how to improve human development, especially in the developing world, with a focus on achieving eight separate, yet linked, goals. Yet, despite the long-running concern at the UN about SHRH, which initially surfaced in the early 1990s, when the MDGs were first announced they did not contain any explicit sexual and reproductive health objective. However, following the Millennium Project's three-year study on implementing the MDGs and a period of considerable activism, the integral link between reproductive health and development as originally set out at Cairo in 1994 was internationally reaffirmed at a MDG-related World Summit meeting in 2005. One reason why SRHRs were not initially mentioned in the MDGs was the lack of consensus about just what these goals would be and how they might be achieved. Finally, in 2008, that is, seven years after the pursuit of the MDGs began and half way toward the 2015 deadline for achieving them, universal access to reproductive health by 2015 became a late, yet obviously highly important, global development target under Goal 5 on Maternal Health.

The main focus in chapter 5 was on another major issue dividing conservatives and liberals at the UN, in relation to how to achieve improved human development outcomes especially among the poorest people in the world's most impoverished countries. We looked at differing views between conservatives and liberals on the right to development and how to achieve this goal, with each highlighting the moral and ethical necessity of advancing the position of the poorest people. The chapter surveyed FBO involvement in formulation and development of the MDGs, a major example of the international community seeking to find ways to deal with a particularly egregious issue: polarization between rich and poor, a key global social justice issue. The main UN case study in chapter 5 was on the initially promising, then increasingly stormy and finally de facto severed relationship between the World Bank and the WCC, which highlighted and explained differing interpretations of what constitutes (human) development and how to improve outcomes in this regard.

Chapter 6 also looked at a key human rights issue at the UN involving FBOs and UN actors: the equally polarizing issue of defamation of religion. It examined differing perspectives evinced by conservative and liberal FBOs and highlighted ideological polarization between two viewpoints: "freedom of expression" *versus* the right of faiths not to be defamed. A key FBO in this context was the OIC—an example, along with the Holy See, of what I identified as an "umbrella FBO," that is, a major UN player that leads and coordinates on an issue, collecting resources, including faith-based and secular entities, to help it achieve its objectives. Defamation of religion was not however simply an issue dividing Islamic FBOs and Muslim-majority states at the UN from the rest. Rather, it was a concern that highlighted the umbrella role of the OIC—which led and coordinated other actors, including: both faith-based and secular actors (including the Russian Orthodox Church and the governments of Russia and China)—in pursuit of a campaign to make critiquing religion against international human rights law. An equally vocal alliance of opponents, both secular and faith-based, fought against the OIC-led campaign, mounting a long-running, apparently successful, operation in opposition to defamation of religion taking priority over freedom of expression.

Examination of these topics in chapters 4, 5, and 6 served to highlight and illustrate significant differences at the UN, between conservative and liberal FBOs, from within shared faith traditions as well as from secular points of view. Overall, chapters 4–6 examined controversial topics at the UN, which generated prolonged debate and discussion involving both FBOs and secular allies but were not definitively resolved. The overall aim was not only to understand how these separate controversies collectively fit into a pattern of conservative *versus* liberal conflict at the UN, but also to highlight, examine, and explain, on the one hand, ideological differences between FBOs and, on the other, to understand their tactics in order to try to achieve their objectives.

Between 58 percent and 75 percent of FBOs registered with ECOSOC are north-based and Christian. This is not to suggest that all of them, or even most of them, work together in pursuit of collective goals, evincing shared ambitions and objectives. In other words, there is no evidence of the nearly 200 Christian FBOs generally working together in a coordinated coalition activity. Instead, something more subtle, yet discernible, goes on at the UN involving Christian FBOs. Most emanate from developed northern (i.e, Western) countries that are themselves well represented in international fora, thus giving "their" FBOs from such countries a *raison d'être* to engage with the UN. This is the key global environment where (nearly) all the world's governments and thousands of secular NGOs from their own national and regional backgrounds are also very well represented compared to southern and non-Christian entities. The UN is where FBOs can relatively easily engage in dialogue and attempt to be influential with secular actors with whom they are likely to be familiar from their domestic and/or regional environments. This represents increased opportunity not only to be influential but also to seek to affect outcomes in a context of cultural familiarity. As suggested by Carrette and Miall (2012), this may also serve to undermine the likelihood of FBOs from different cultural contexts making their mark at the UN: "The international political system is a development of the Judaeo-Christian beliefs" that favors certain types of faith and FBOs. In addition, despite the large and growing number of FBOs at the UN, including highly influential umbrella entities, such as the Holy See and the Organization of Islamic Cooperation, there is a long-established, still for the most part extant, convention at the UN, "not to talk about religion, and not to talk in religious terms" (ibid.) The UN epitomizes the kind of international political system that Carrette and Miall (2012) have in mind when they talk of today's international political system as a system that developed from a foundation of "Judaeo-Christian beliefs." Key among these are the values of the UN: the rule of law, democracy, and individual human rights, cornerstone of the international states system from its inception after the wars of religion in Europe that came to an end in the mid-seventeenth century, marked by the Peace of

Westphalia in 1648 and subsequent development of a secular system based on Judaeo-Christian beliefs. This goes to the heart of the matter and is suggested by the following question: How and why do FBOs interact with each other and with secular actors at the UN, and with what results? To do this, FBOs must be willing to "sign up" to the UN's liberal and secular values, in order to gain entry into debates and discussions at the UN and to try to influence outcomes. The point is that to be seen and heard—successfully and purposively—at the UN, FBOs *must* accord with the organization's secular, liberal, and irreligious values, norms, and beliefs, and this privileges those northern, Christian FBOs, whose key concerns, values, norms, and related goals come from similar foundations. This reminds us that when assessing the impact of FBOs at the UN, it is important to bear in mind that the UN is a demonstrably secular organization, founded after 1945 on nonreligious values but whose cultural makeup involves values derived from foundational Judaeo-Christian beliefs, which, after becoming secularized, today underpin and reflect the characteristics and global spread of a post-Westphalia, West-directed and focused international order (Haynes, Hough, Malik, and Pettiford, 2011).

There is nothing natural or inevitable about the secular character and philosophy of the UN. It is an ideological choice, whose adoption stems from the concerns prevalent after the defeat of fascism and Nazism in 1945, and the corresponding creation and development of an international order founded on secularized, Judaeo-Christian human rights and individualist interpretations and values, as marked and symbolized by the 1948 UN Human Rights Charter. The UN was founded in an era of postwar international relations where faith-based values were not an important or overt aspect of the secular and individualistic norms and values underpinning the framework for what was hoped to be a more cooperative world order following the devastation and ideological polarization of World War II. It is this background and the values to which it gave birth that explains the secular ethos of the UN, which still endures six decades later. This assertion is evidenced by the otherwise inexplicable comments of a senior adviser to the UN secretary general just a handful of years ago. In 2008, there was a conversation, reported by the international relations scholar Elizabeth Shakman Hurd, between John Gerard Ruggie, at the time special representative of the UN secretary general for Business and Human Rights and his Harvard University colleague Father Bryan Hehir, Catholic priest and secretary for Health Care and Social Services in the Archdiocese of Boston. In response to Hehir's question asking where religion is to be found and where is it influential at the UN, Ruggie replied saying that "there is none [that is, no religion] at the UN." As the book has made repeatedly clear, however, there is actually *much* religion at the UN, especially in the form of FBOs, as well as several states, including Iran and Saudi Arabia, whose faith input, from several faith traditions, is an important and arguably growing component of what the UN does in relation to various justice and human rights concerns.

FBOs compete with each other primarily on ideational—not theological—grounds. This implies that, for example, socially conservative FBOs may well work not only with theologically conservative FBOs but also socially conservative secular state and non-state actors at the UN. On the other hand, liberal FBOs will frequently work not only with other liberal FBOs but also with liberal NGOs and governments, in pursuit of their goals. In short, FBOs wishing to maximize their influence at the UN typically seek to link up with allies—including other

FBOs, secular NGOs, and friendly governments, which share their ideological—not necessarily theological—norms, values, and beliefs. Since the 1990s, the UN has focused on a range of justice and human rights concerns, and such issues have collectively been a key reason why many FBOs see the UN as a source of increasingly authoritative decision making that often impacts upon global public policy and, as a result, can influence what occurs within states.

Some FBOs active at the UN manage to achieve persistent influence, such as the Holy See, via regularized and/or institutionalized access to opinion formers and decision makers located in friendly governments and intergovernmental organizations. Note that we have defined and operationalized the concept of FBO in a wider way than is usually the case in the literature. Rather than functioning as a virtual synonym of the secular NGO, we have seen that there is a second—but not secondary—type of FBO at the UN, whose activities as important umbrella entities are manifested in their important roles as coalition-building entities, which come together in pursuit of individual campaigns on issues of shared importance. Key examples of these umbrella FBOs at the UN are the Holy See, the WCC, and the OIC. Their leading role in relation to various justice and human rights campaigns does not imply a faith *versus* secular approach at the UN; rather, it highlights shared ideological campaigns based on shared sets of ideas reflecting shared political and social objectives for which both faith-based and secular entities—both state and non-state—can agree to work together and coordinate their activities, often via the good offices of umbrella FBOs.

On the other hand, less successful FBOs are characterized by their lack of consistent capacity to enjoy consistent access to public opinion formers and influential networks at the UN. As a result they typically lack much influence and leverage on global public policy. The conclusion from this is that to be influential at the UN as a FBO, you need to be willing to network widely, and work with a variety of actors whose makeup can differ from issue to issue and topic to topic. You need to be flexible and pragmatic and willing to accept that you won't necessarily get all—or perhaps even many—of the goals that you pursue. You will need to realize that the world is not especially linked to faith understandings or see that the pursuit of resolution to pressing concerns depends on more and better expressions of faith. Instead, the pursuit of various sets of ideational goals and values needs to take account of what other, including non-faith-based actors are doing, and be willing to link faith-based values to their maybe secular goals.

Finally, what of the future in relation to FBOs at the UN? To what extent does widespread religious resurgence and development of what is sometimes called postsecular international relations suggest that the influence of FBOs will grow at the UN in the medium term and beyond? On the one hand, it is very difficult to assert with confidence that the UN is getting more oriented to faith *per se*. Given that FBOs seem more likely to achieve objectives when they are willing to be flexible and pragmatic and work with a variety of entities in order to achieve faith-*linked* but not faith-*rooted* goals in relation to justice and human rights at the UN, it would be wrong to say that we are seeing the unraveling of a secular international system that has been in place in its current form since 1945 but has its roots in developments since the mid-seventeenth century. On the other hand, it would be difficult to ignore evidence manifested in various ways at the UN in recent years—including growing numbers and increasingly high profiles of some FBOs such as the Holy See and the OIC, apparent willingness of once doggedly secular entities such as the World Bank and the IMF to converse with faith-based entities as equals, undeniably individually high profiles of certain faith leaders, and a more general increase in concern with both ethical and moral issues at the UN—to assert that somehow the influence of faith is declining. Instead, what has emerged from the pages of this book is that "modern" FBOs—that is, those that are pragmatic, flexible, and goal-oriented and willing to work with a variety of entities, both faith-based and secular, to try to achieve their objectives, may represent an emerging type of actor in international relations that, taking advantage of opportunities offered by globalization and the willingness of IGOs such as the UN to take their views seriously, are now able to pursue their goals in a context that regularly sees assertion of the priority of ethically informed international relations, with associated justice and human rights goals.

Notes

1 Faith-Based Organizations at the United Nations

1. The Oxford Dictionary defines "faith" as involving "strong belief in the doctrines of a body of ideas, which might be religiously-based or secular, based on spiritual conviction rather than proof." (http://www.oxforddictionaries. com/definition/english/faith).

2. Tadros (2010: 5, fn. 9) seeks to differentiate between what he terms "Muslim FBOs," which he characterizes as engaging with "Islam as a spiritual religion" and "Islamic FBOs" "that follow a more political-religious engagement." However, Tadros does not provide examples of the different FBOs that he has in mind, and I am not persuaded that the division between "spiritual" and "political-religious" "Islamic" FBOs is a defensible or useful one. In this book, I shall refer solely to Islamic FBOs—in recognition of the fact that to contribute to debates and, more generally, to interact at the UN it is necessarily for FBOs to engage with both "political-religious" issues, as well as "spiritual" concerns.

3. Some scholars, such as Katherine Marshall (2013: 1), writing about faith in development, prefer "faith-*inspired* organization" (FIO) to "faith-*based* organization." Marshall notes that

many FIOs are uncomfortable with the term FBO when they argue that they are "inspired" by a faith tradition, not "based" in it. This is because they feel that "faith-based" makes such organizations sound as though what they do is explicitly based on the wishes of a specific faith community, whereas FIO "capture[s] a wider group of organizations. FIOs also are advocates and service providers."

4. The term "Holy See" is from the Latin *Sancta Sedes*, meaning "holy chair."

5. By 2013, the number of NGOs with formal consultative status with ECOSOC had grown to 3,735, an increase, compared to 2008, of 17 percent. The most up-to-date list of ECOSOC-registered NGOs, including FBOs, which are not counted in a separate listing or category in the PDF, is dated April 5, 2013. The full list is available at http://csonet.org/content/documents/E2012INF6.pdf (last accessed June 23, 2014).

6. The author of the current book was the academic consultant for the project (http://www.kent.ac.uk/secl/thrs/research/ahrc.html).

7. Bryan Hehir is Parker Gilbert Montgomery Professor of the Practice of Religion and Public Life at Harvard University. John Gerard Ruggie is Berthold Beitz Professor in Human Rights and International Affairs at Harvard's Kennedy School of Government and affiliated professor in International Legal Studies at Harvard Law School. Ruggie served as United Nations assistant secretary-general for Strategic Planning from 1997 to 2001, a post created specifically for him by then UN secretary-general, Kofi Annan. In 2005, responding to a request by the UN Commission on Human Rights (now Human Rights Council), Annan appointed Ruggie as the secretary-general's special representative for Business and Human Rights, a post he held under Secretary-General Ban Ki-Moon until 2011. Ruggie's main task was to propose measures to strengthen the human rights performance of the business sector around the world. (http://www.hks.harvard.edu/m-rcbg/johnruggie/index.html).

8. "UN values" highlight the value and importance of democracy, good governance, and human rights. For details,

see http://www.un.org/en/globalissues/democracy/ Last accessed May 28, 2013.

9. Today, there are 193 members of the UN. The most recent is South Sudan, admitted into the UN in July 2011.

2 Religious Resurgence and Postsecular International Relations

1. Resacralization refers to the return of religious meanings to the public realm, including in relation to politics, the arts, and resistance to secularization, especially from religious believers.

2. An episteme is a set of linked ideas that, taken together, serve to provide the basis of the knowledge that is widely believed to be intellectually certain at a particular era or epoch.

3. The literature typically refers to the return of "religion" not "faith" to international relations, and I shall follow that usage in this section.

4. A "UN System Organizational Chart" is reproduced at http://www.un.org/en/aboutun/structure/pdfs/un-system-chart-color-sm.pdf. Last accessed May 24, 2013.

5. FBOs and other religious actors are rarely accorded much attention in discussions of global public policy. For example, Stone's (2008) wide-ranging and widely cited article on global public policy includes not one reference to "religion" or "faith." Between publication in 2008 and that in mid-2013, Stone's article had garnered nearly 100 citations. Yet her ignoring of FBOs and religion more generally is not an isolated aberration. This is underlined by the fact that the flagship journal on global governance, *Global Governance*, featured *no* articles concerned with "religion" or "faith" between 2004 and 2013. See http://journals.rienner.com/toc/ggov/19/2 for list of articles over 2004–2013. Last accessed May 28, 2013.

6. The Charter of the UN, including the Preamble, are reproduced at the International Court of Justice website: http://www.icj-cij.org/documents/index.php?p1=4&p2=1&p3=0.

7. In 2013, the Committee of Religious NGOs is an institutionalized entity that produces an annual report of

activity and has 38 different religious groups as members, including Christian, Jewish, Bahá'í, Buddhist, Hindu, and Zoroastrian entities. There are no Muslim members. (http://rngos.wordpress.com/member-organizations/).

8. "The NGO Committee on Spirituality, Values, and Global Concerns (NY) envisions a global culture of peace based on justice, solidarity, inclusiveness, shared responsibility, harmony, cooperation, compassion, love, wisdom, goodwill and reverence for the sacredness of all life through active peaceful engagement." (http://www.csvgc-ny.org/).

3   Faith-Based Organizations at the United Nations: Theory and Practice

1. The present author was academic consultant for the Carrette /Miall project.

2. I use the term "transnational civil society" rather than "global civil society," as the latter term implies a universal reach that may be lacking in such networks.

3. But for FBOs this is not a constant but differs greatly depending on the size/finances/organizational capacity of a FBO.

4. "The smallest sovereign state in the world; the see of the Pope (as the Bishop of Rome); home of the Pope and the central administration of the Roman Catholic Church; achieved independence from Italy in 1929" (http://wordnetweb. princeton.edu/perl/webwn?s=holy see).

5. Interviews with representatives of two religious human rights organizations. One organization had been consistently denied consultative status (Ottawa, September 2000) and one organization had recently seen its consultative status revoked (Zurich, October 2000). (from Bush PhD).

6. CFC describes its mission as "to shape and advance sexual and reproductive ethics that are based on justice, reflect a commitment to women's well-being and respect and affirm the capacity of women and men to make moral decisions about their lives. CFC works in the United States and internationally to ensure that all people have access to safe

and affordable reproductive health-care services and to infuse our core values into public policy, community life and Catholic social teaching and thinking." CFC writes that they "are part of the great majority who believes that Catholic teachings on conscience mean that every individual must follow his or her own conscience—and respect others' right to do the same" (http://www.catholicsforchoice.org/about/ourwork/default.asp).

4   Women's Sexual and Reproductive Health Rights

1. "For 50 years, the Religious Action Center of Reform Judaism ('the RAC') has been the hub of Jewish social justice and legislative activity in Washington, D.C. As the DC office of the Union for Reform Judaism, the RAC educates and mobilizes the Reform Jewish community on legislative and social concerns, advocating on more than 70 different issues, including economic justice, civil rights, religious liberty, Israel and more. As a 501c3 non-profit organization, the RAC's advocacy work is completely non-partisan and pursues public policies that reflect the Jewish values of social justice that form the core of our mandate." (http://rac.org/aboutrac/).
2. Seeing mutual benefit in working together via a shared concern with "pro-family values," the "Baptist-burqa" coalition manage to endure, overcoming such setbacks as 9/11, whose impact otherwise was to divide the Christian and Muslim worlds from each other.
3. As Association of United Families International, UFI has had special consultative status with ECOSOC since 1999.
4. For a full list of members, go to: http://ecumenicalwomen.org/about/.
5. Details of the Istanbul meeting are at http://www.unfpa.org/culture/docs/global_forum_summary.pdf Last accessed June 13, 2014.
6. Details at http://www.unfpa.org/webdav/site/global/shared/documents/publications/2009/global_forums_fbo.pdf) Last accessed May 28, 2013.

5   International Development and the Millennium Development Goals

1. UN agencies concerned with human development include: UN Department of Economic and Social Affairs, the UN Population Fund, Joint UN Program on HIV/AIDS, UN Children's Fund, UN Alliance of Civilizations, UN Development Program, UN Environmental Program, UN Education and Science Organization, UN Human Settlements Program, UN Office for Partnerships, UN Women, the World Health Organization, and the World Bank.

2. http://hdr.undp.org/en/humandev for definitions.

3. There is a notable exception to this general rule. The UNDP has sought to emphasize *human economic development* in a broadly defined sense.

4. The full list of MDGs is at http://www.un.org/millenniumgoals/. Last accessed June 14, 2014.

5. Joshi and O'Dell (2013) do not classify the World Bank as a UN agency. The UN itself describes the World Bank as an "autonomous organization linked to the UN through [a] special agreement," via the "coordinating machinery" of ECOSOC. For details of the bank's relationship with the UN over time, see http://www.un.org/Overview/uninbrief/institutions.shtml. Last accessed June 14, 2014.

6. Member churches are listed at http://www.oikoumene.org/en/member-churches/list. Last accessed June 14, 2014.

6   Human Rights and "Defamation of Religion"

1. This publication "was the product of Religion Counts, an internationally recognized group of scholars and experts organized to provide religious perspectives in the development of international public policy. Religion Counts [was] convened by The Park Ridge Center for the Study of Health, Faith, and Ethics and Catholics for a Free Choice"

(http://www.catholicsforchoice.org/topics/politics/documen
ts/2000religionandpublicpolicyatheun.pdf).

2. The 12 "religious states" are: Afghanistan, Bahrain, Brunei,
   Iran, Maldives, Mauritania, Oman, Pakistan, Saudi Arabia,
   Sudan, Yemen (all Muslim-majority), and the Holy See
   (Roman Catholic).

3. The 15 are: Algeria, Bangladesh, Comoros, Djibouti, Egypt,
   Iraq, Jordan, Kuwait, Libya, Malaysia, Morocco, Qatar,
   Somalia, Tunisia, and United Arab Emirates.

4. The 20 are: Azerbaijan, Burkina Faso, Chad, Guinea,
   Kazakhstan, Kosovo, Kyrgyzstan, Mali, Niger, Senegal,
   Tajikistan, Turkey, Turkmenistan, Albania, The Gambia,
   Indonesia, Lebanon, Sierra Leone, Syria, and Uzbekistan.

5. The HRC comprises 47 member states, elected by the
   majority of members of the general assembly via direct
   and secret ballot. The general assembly takes into account
   the candidate states' contribution to the promotion and
   protection of human rights, as well as their voluntary pledges
   and commitments in this regard. Council members serve for
   a period of three years and are not eligible for immediate
   reelection after serving two consecutive terms. The council's
   membership is based on equitable geographical distribution.
   Seats are distributed as follows: (1) African States: 13 seats (2)
   Asia-Pacific States: 13 seats (3) Latin American and Caribbean
   States: 8 seats (4) Western European and other States: 7 seats,
   and (5) Eastern European States: 6 seats (http://www.ohchr
   .org/EN/HRBodies/HRC/Pages/Membership.aspx).

6. International Covenant on Civil and Political Rights is at
   http://www.ohchr.org/en/professionalinterest/pages/ccpr
   .aspx. Accessed June 20, 2014.

7. Ahmadis were declared by the Muslim World League to be
   apostates in a *fatwa* in 1974 (Yohanan Friedmann. *Prophecy
   Continuous. Aspects of Ahmadi Religious Thought and Its Medieval
   Background.* Oxford University Press, New Delhi. p. 44.).

8. http://www.unwatch.org/site/apps/nlnet/content2.aspx?c
   =bdKKISNqEmG&b=1330815&ct=6859557 The Israel-based
   "UN Watch," initiated the "Joint NGO Statement on Danger
   of U.N. 'Defamation of Religions' Campaign." (http://www

.unwatch.org/site/apps/nlnet/content2.aspx?c=bdKKISNqE
mG&b=1330815&ct=).

9. The First Amendment guarantees freedoms concerning
religion, expression, assembly, and the right to petition. It
forbids Congress from both promoting one religion over
others and also restricting an individual's religious practices.
The First Amendment also guarantees freedom of expression
by prohibiting Congress from restricting the press or the
rights of individuals to speak freely. Finally, it guarantees
the right of citizens to assemble peacefully and to petition
the government (http://www.law.cornell.edu/constitution
/first_amendment).

Index

international non-governmental
    organizations (INGOs), 40
International Youth Coalition, 97–8
Iran, 25, 38, 43, 144, 147, 156, 159,
    165, 177
Islam and Islamic FBOs, 3, 5, 18, 21,
    32, 40, 41, 42, 76, 79, 123, 140,
    145, 151, 174, 181n2
    See also Muslims
Islamic Relief, 22, 123, 150, 169
Israel, 22, 43, 170
Istanbul Process, 160
    See also defamation of religion

Judaeo-Christian beliefs, 24, 141, 145,
    165, 167, 171, 175, 176
Judaism and Jewish FBOs, 18, 21, 22,
    32, 98, 123, 151, 157, 169, 170–1
Jyllands-Posten, 141
    See also "Danish cartoons"
    controversy

Karam, Azza, 25, 26–7, 44
Kozik, US Ambassador Michael G.,
    163–4

Lead Us Not into Temptation
    (World Council of Churches
    publication), 131
Lesbian, Gay, Bisexual, and
    Transgender (LGBT) issues, 104

Marshall, Katherine, 128
Millennium Development Goals, 6,
    7, 16, 26, 59, 84, 109, 113–37,
    140, 172
multinational corporations, 114, 116
Muslim Brotherhood, 12, 35, 149
Muslim World League, 4, 79, 146,
    148–9, 152, 156, 187n7
Muslims, 21, 23, 32, 79, 93, 104, 141,
    145, 165
    See also Islam and Islamic FBOs

National Right to Life Committee, 97
natural environment, 57, 68, 115

Non-governmental Committee
    on Spirituality, Values,
    and Global Concerns,
    47, 184n8
non-governmental organizations,
    'secular' 20, 23, 54, 62
non-governmental organizations
    and faith-based organizations,
    theoretical approaches to
    understanding, 69–74
Norway, 106, 148, 152

Obama, Barack, 159, 161, 162
Office of the United Nations High
    Commissioner for Human
    Rights, 164
Organization of Islamic Cooperation
    (OIC), 13, 15, 16, 17, 20, 23, 25,
    34, 41, 55, 69, 74–80, 139, 140,
    144–65, 174, 175, 178, 179

Pakistan, 102, 104, 105, 141, 144, 147,
    154, 155–6, 159, 163, 165
Peace of Westphalia (1648), 38, 39, 44,
    175–6
postsecular/postsecularism, 24,
    29–50, 59
poverty (alleviation), 111, 112, 114,
    115, 117, 118–19, 121, 122, 131

Reform Judaism, 100
Religious Action Center of Reform
    Judaism, 185n1
religious "deprivatization," 53, 54
religious international
    nongovernmental organizations
    (RINGOs), 7, 8
religious non-governmental
    organisations (RNGOs), 3, 7,
    8, 56
religious resurgence, 2, 28, 29–50, 48,
    53, 168, 171
Roman Catholic Church, 13, 16, 34,
    40, 41, 78, 184n4
Roman Catholics, 14
Rudolph, Susanne Hueber, 34, 35

Printed and bound in the United States of America